REVOLUTIONIZE™
Your Corporate Life

My take on the book is pretty simple. The book isn't for everyone. I see an increasing number of people who want success but can't manage the stress of day-to-day life, reach the balance between work and home, or just can't get in the proper mindset to achieve success. However, if someone has decided to make real changes in their life, and they've mentally cleared the deck and are looking for a simple yet solid path to follow, this book is a great guide. Congrats!

—**Tom Pierce**, President,
Frontier Marketing & Management

I recently engaged Peggy's help in coaching a colleague at work. The results have been outstanding with positive changes realized in a short period of time. Peggy has a gift in her ability to enlighten others in order to improve their lives. She has found her calling in life.

—**Rob Bailey**, Senior Director, Domtar Corporation

When you set out in this world you are basically on your own trying to figure things out. Most of the time we learn through trial and error how to be successful at work and at home. After twenty-five years in my career I finally found a valid approach to help me professionally and personally. *Revolutionize Your Corporate Life* provides a concrete plan of action that anyone can do if he/she truly wishes to improve their life. Through implementation of these techniques I made significant, positive changes in my career and in myself. I continue to apply the information on a daily basis as the practices can be honed and used again and again for added success and growth.

—**Melissa Mulhollan**,
High school teacher and mother of two

My leadership team and I were about to create a set of action plans to launch the new campus strategic plan. To be more effective in the execution of our plan, I decided to hold a leadership retreat, and I invited Peggy Caruso to act as our facilitator. It turns out that was one of the best decisions I made. She conducted several interviews with me to solidify the goals and outcomes of the retreat and then built a customized half-day session with activities designed to improve communication and team-building. The retreat was a success, and we are now one year into the plan and making great progress.

— **Melanie L. Hatch**, PhD,
Chancellor, Penn State DuBois

As a small business owner I fell into the trap of not being able to compartmentalize my life. When I was involved in what should be a relaxing activity I was thinking about work, and while working I was never fully immersed in the task at hand. After coaching with Peggy, I am amazed when I reflect back on the positive changes in my life. I have a focus, positive attitude, and passion about myself, my family, my career, and my business. Peggy does not make decisions for you but instead helps you develop ways to deal with situations using your own knowledge, self-awareness, and, most important, positive energy. I am a firm believer in not only the principles that Peggy teaches, but in how to effectively implement them as lasting positive changes in your everyday life. Anyone, no matter where you are in your life, your career, or your relationship, will benefit from what Peggy has to offer.

— **Mike Buerk**, Summit Consulting Services

REVOLUTIONIZE™
Your Corporate Life

A Simple Guide to Leadership,
Balance, and Success in Your Business

PEGGY CARUSO

NEW YORK

NASHVILLE • MELBOURNE • VANCOUVER

REVOLUTIONIZE™ Your Corporate Life
A Simple Guide to Leadership, Balance, and Success in Your Business

© 2017 **PEGGY CARUSO**

Published in New York, New York, by Morgan James Publishing. Morgan James and The Entrepreneurial Publisher are trademarks of Morgan James, LLC.
www.MorganJamesPublishing.com

The Morgan James Speakers Group can bring authors to your live event. For more information or to book an event visit The Morgan James Speakers Group at www.TheMorganJamesSpeakersGroup.com.

Shelfie

A free eBook edition is available
with the purchase of this print book.

CLEARLY PRINT YOUR NAME ABOVE IN UPPER CASE

Instructions to claim your free eBook edition:
1. Download the Shelfie app for Android or iOS
2. Write your name in **UPPER CASE** above
3. Use the Shelfie app to submit a photo
4. Download your eBook to any device

ISBN 978-1-68350-187-9 paperback
ISBN 978-1-68350-188-6 eBook
ISBN 978-1-68350-189-3 hardcover
Library of Congress Control Number:
2016913821

Cover Design by:
Rachel Lopez
www.r2cdesign.com

Interior Design by:
Bonnie Bushman
The Whole Caboodle Graphic Design

In an effort to support local communities, raise awareness and funds, Morgan James Publishing donates a percentage of all book sales for the life of each book to Habitat for Humanity Peninsula and Greater Williamsburg.

Get involved today! Visit
www.MorganJamesBuilds.com

FOR MY FRIEND...

I believe the dedication of a book is very important. It places emphasis on a person who has made a significant impact in your life. With that being said, I dedicate this book to someone who has played a major role in my life. I have always been very focused in my professional career; however, there are times we become challenged or disoriented with a direction. On this particular journey I lost sight of something very important within myself. I am fortunate to be surrounded by so many wonderful people in my life, and everyone made multiple attempts to guide me in a direction to overcome an obstacle that was delaying the completion of my book.

Frustration was making it more difficult, so one night I reached out to an old friend with the intent to clear my head. Upon expressing concern for my challenge, she went straight to the core of my being—my heart. She forced me to go deep inside of myself and helped me come to the realization that in the corporate world we tend to get caught up in the business realm of things. While being confronted with multiple business decisions, I wasn't able to differentiate how it was affecting me from an emotional standpoint.

This individual is my dear friend of thirteen years, Shannon Oakes. She is a successful business owner of a restaurant (The West Wind) located in the small town of St. Marys, PA. Shannon has worked for me in several businesses, but she is so much more than an employee. She is a very dear friend of the heart. I mentored her, and she has successfully applied all that she has learned and continues to educate herself in new areas. This growth has created a new state of awareness that has allowed her to successfully apply the principles contained in this book.

With the effective application of my mentoring program, she was able to provide direction to assist me with self-awareness. We all become complacent at certain times in our lives, and sometimes that complacency causes us to become unbalanced, which can cause lack of focus. Shannon was able to take corporate principles and incorporate an emotional awareness. Thank you, my dear friend, for never losing sight of what is most important. I love you and am grateful for your friendship.

Table of Contents

Foreword

Welcome to the Revolutionize series and, specifically, to *Revolutionize Your Corporate Life*.

To revolutionize your life, it all starts with you, the most important person in the world. Are you willing to change and develop and excel in your personal and professional life?

If not, don't waste your money or time on this book, or any book for that matter.

This book will help you recognize what needs to be changed, discover where the behavior comes from, and then take the necessary steps to accelerate change. The end result: you will become a better person. You will eliminate negativity, worry, fear, and doubt and replace them with positivity. You will have courage, motivation, and persistence, and you will develop your intuition.

Don't worry; Peggy has it all covered for you in this book.

As an eight-time entrepreneur, along with being an executive and personal development coach, Peggy believes as I do that your personal and professional life go hand-in-hand, from the inside out!

Whether the desire is to change your career, excel in the corporate world, become an entrepreneur, or assist you in personal development, *Revolutionize Your Corporate Life* provides you with the tools for a new direction or will simply heighten your awareness for positive growth.

Attitude and personal leadership are foundational to your success. It is very important for you to realize how personal leadership skills can make you stronger when you are faced with challenges. Let's not forget, life itself is a challenge.

Revolutionize Your Corporate Life will give you the necessary leadership skills, from effective communication to time and stress management, from career and family balance to making decisions and setting goals—personal and professional, short term and long term. Again, it all starts with you!

You will experience a personal and corporate paradigm shift that takes you quantum leaps forward with courage and confidence. You will achieve your desired outcome.

Revolutionize Your Corporate Life now!

Bob Urichuck
Founder of the Velocity Selling System, international speaker and trainer, and author of three books. Ranked in the world's top 10 sales gurus since 2008

Audio Foreword

By Bob Proctor, International bestselling author
and star of *The Secret*

It's a real pleasure for me to be working with Peggy Caruso. Peggy has spent years studying human personality—studying why we do what we do and why we don't do many of the things we want to do. We've got deep reservoirs of talent and ability within us. *Revolutionize Your Life* and *Revolutionize Your Child's Life* enable you to set aside some of those things you're just so tired of doing, so tired of putting up with, to let the genius flow to the surface and manifest in results in your life.

I want to congratulate you for making a wise decision of getting involved in Peggy's program. Revolutionize Your Life will definitely do exactly what it says. Begin to live as you like by no longer living as you dislike. Peggy is a wise leader. She's a great career and personal development coach, so sit back, relax, and listen very carefully. But understand one thing: listening to something is one thing; acting on it is another. It's through repetition, listening over and over again, that you begin to alter that conditioning that rests deep in the treasury of your subconscious. You'll begin acting on it, and that's when your life will truly be revolutionized. This is Bob Proctor. Now sit back and get involved.

To hear the audio go to: www.lifecoachingandbeyond.com

Acknowledgments

This book contains not only helpful information to the reader, but my life's passion. I love providing useful information to people on a personal and professional level. My previous book, *Revolutionize Your Child's Life*, was intended to provide preventative measures for parents relative to societal challenges. This book contains useful information for those of you in the corporate world. Although that is the intent, there is valuable information to assist anyone trying to balance their corporate world with home life. Many people have inspired me to pursue my present career and write this book.

Boundless thanks to Bob Proctor, international bestselling author, who made me realize where my true passions lie and how to bring them all to the surface with the intent of changing lives. A very special thank-you for the audio foreword for my "Revolutionize" book series: *Revolutionize Your Life*, *Revolutionize Your Child's Life*, and *Revolutionize Your Corporate Life*. His teachings reinforce my inner strength and provide the faith to persevere. The kindness he extends is a direct reflection of the principles he teaches.

A special thank-you to my dear friend Bob Urichuck for writing the foreword of this book. We were in a great mastermind team together, the International Brain Trust. He is the founder of the Velocity Selling System, an international speaker and trainer, author of three books, and ranked among the top-10 sales gurus since 2008.

Dr. Steve G. Jones, who encourages his students to pursue their dreams. He passionately presents the necessary tools to help you reach success.

Dr. Robert Anthony, for educating me about the subconscious mind and for his wonderful program "The Secret of Deliberate Creation." Sharing his teachings of the different periods in a child's life has certainly made a difference.

Apart from the above, in the course of my studies and while writing this book, numerous people have inspired me with their vision and understanding of higher education. Several personal acquaintances have shared their knowledge, guidance, and heart with no expectations.

I would also like to thank the following for assisting me at every level of my book: Morgan James Publishing Company, which has gone above and beyond with guidance and support. Their team is a valuable asset to the publication of my book.

A special thank-you to David Hancock, Jim Howard, Margo Toulouse, Bethany Marshall, and Angie Kiesling.

Thank you to everyone who wrote a heartfelt testimonial. Your words mean so much to me. You are my inspiration. Also, to my team and friends: Dee Petraitis, Jenn Marsico, Neil Hanes and Melissa Mulhollan. We are on an amazing journey together.

My dear friend and business owner Shannon Oakes, who helped me with my vision while writing. She inspired me to continue when I became overwhelmed. Thank you, Shannon!

A very special thank-you to my mother and best friend, Mary Ellen Bolitiski. She supports and loves me through all my endeavors. Her love is unconditional, and she has always been a true inspiration in my life.

To my wonderful children, Nicole and Joshua, who are amazing and make me so proud. They are a direct reflection of what I teach. My daughter, Nicole is so well balanced with raising a family and having a career. Her husband, Chris is a wonderful addition to our family and I am very lucky to have him as a son-in-law. My son, Joshua is career driven and will positively incorporate that same balance with family someday. Thank you to Kelly for the love you give my son and the happiness you bring to our family.

My very special grandson, Jordan, who continually makes me smile. His kindness and sincerity have already proven to be a success in his life. Persistence resonates within him relative to academics and sports.

Bob Hallstrom, who has been my very best and true friend throughout. He continually supports and believes in me and has been my sounding board and a true inspiration. He has reached success at many levels and is a perfect example for those who are seeking balance in the corporate realm. I am excited to be on a wonderful journey together. Determination, willpower, imagination, and goals are at the forefront of his plan of action, and being an architect allows him to focus on details, which is a key component in the corporate world.

To all the wonderful clients who work so hard to achieve their own success and continually make positive changes. I am very grateful for everyone who has gone through my program. They come into the program as new clients and leave it as dear friends.

I am happy and grateful to all of you . . . God bless each of you!

Introduction

Why did I write this book, and why is it part of my "REVOLUTIONIZE" series?

To revolutionize your life at any level means to transform/change, develop, and then excel you to personal and professional transformation. There are many stages and principles that require application. This book will help you recognize what needs to be changed, discover where the behavior comes from, and then take the necessary steps to accelerate change. Let me be clear about something: it is very difficult to implement this procedure; however, once you desire that change, I can offer you the necessary tools to propel you toward exponential growth.

As an eight-time entrepreneur and executive and personal development coach, I believe your personal and professional life go hand-in-hand. Whether you desire to change your career, excel in the corporate world, become an entrepreneur, or grow through personal development, this book will provide the tools for a new direction or heighten your awareness for positive growth.

The following is a brief synopsis of the chapter material:

Maximize Your Leadership

It does not matter what direction you choose for your life; leadership is the foundation of success relative to personal or professional growth. It is very important for you to realize how leadership skills can make you stronger when you are faced with challenges. Life itself is a challenge.

Learning how to become motivated will help you build a strong team that can recognize where the obstacles are and then envision and plan for the solution. Motivated people are generally happier and more energetic, and they see positive results in their minds.

Many factors come into play, such as effective communication. To communicate effectively you must fully understand the different personalities you are continually confronted with. You need to be able to identify problematic areas and personality differences to create a positive team-building experience. To understand those personalities effectively, you must become aware of each person's representational system and learn how to fully use your senses—the two combined will provide you with effective communication relative to personality traits.

A leader is defined by many things, and it is my hope that the information contained in this book will help you change your behavior, enhance your strengths, and recognize the behavioral patterns of everyone you are associated with. I will also provide information relative to a six-point program on becoming an effective leader. Once you discover the importance of leadership you will see how the remaining information in this book will work in accordance with the leadership role.

In a leadership role, you are faced with many negatives, and one of the setbacks is controlling time and stress. This is not just about controlling the stress for you as the leader, but assisting with every personality that you come in contact with, both personally and professionally.

Identify problematic areas and then begin to manage your time and stress . . .

Manage Your Time And Stress— Not The Other Way Around

Time management is about managing life. It is the analysis of how working hours are spent and the prioritization of tasks in order to maximize personal efficiency in the workplace. Well ... where does that begin?

One of the most important elements of managing stress is decluttering your mind. Once you discover the importance of that calmness, you will enhance your organizational skills.

There are many steps you must take to rid yourself of time and stress issues. One common area is having the ability to set boundaries. This is very difficult for most people—especially on a personal level. In this chapter you will gain insight on how to do that in a professional manner.

Once we encounter time and stress issues we recognize how they limit our ability to persist in a positive manner, and the inevitable happens—PROCRASTINATION. Procrastination holds us hostage in personal and professional growth. If you can recognize what creates that lack of persistence you can then comprehend how to turn it around and utilize it for motivation. All the chapters in this book coincide with success principles and how they are applicable at different levels. For instance, in the first chapter I discuss effective communication on a leadership level, and in chapter two I correlate that same principle with time and stress. There are multiple explanations at different levels.

So, what is stress?

Stress is the physical, chemical, or emotional reaction to the ever increasing demands of life that cause bodily or mental unrest. I will provide you with the symptoms and the solutions. Stress can be caused by multiple things, but fear, worry, and doubt are huge culprits. You must learn how to eliminate them to achieve success and happiness. That is why I continually state that personal and professional go hand-in-hand. Your personal and professional lives are mutually connected. Once you learn how to identify your stressors, you can take the necessary steps to eliminate them.

You then need to find the balance between the two . . .

Hand-In-Hand: Balancing Career And Family

The smallest changes produce the strongest impacts. I love that statement because most people associate change with intensity, and even though I discuss exponential growth, you must realize that when it comes to differentiating between family and career, the smallest changes will have the biggest effect on all aspects of your life.

I discuss the keys to transformation that connect personal and professional. Once you understand the importance of these keys and how to apply them so that you can achieve happiness, you then back those changes with your attitude. Many people bypass the importance of an attitude, which is a composite of your thoughts, feelings, and actions. Attitude alone can create significant results.

People often feel guilty when separating the personal and professional, but in order for you to find balance you MUST be able to identify when and how. There are so many benefits to discovering that balance to bring success to your career and happiness to your personal life.

Many people have guilt about working and leaving children with a caregiver. That also requires balance, so learning effective decision making will provide solutions for a happy and healthy home environment.

Life is all about balance, and that is why I love coaching. Once you find that balance you can make sound decisions . . .

The Decisive Leader

One of the greatest skills a leader can have is the ability to make effective business decisions. Learning that effectiveness will aid in being able to make quick decisions as well. Making sound decisions provides opportunity and allows you to identify the situations that could otherwise be classified as missed opportunity, which stem from fear. Being indecisive can cripple you, and it is imperative that you recognize the difference. I discuss the mistakes that will occur if you are unable to make sound decisions and then educate on the process of turning it into a positive situation.

Decision makers are not afraid of fear. They know they can learn from their negative experiences. Failure is a steppingstone to success, and we become successful from those setbacks. People who can make sound decisions have a strong self-image and a high degree of self-esteem.

I will also teach about self-actualization, or the achievement of one's full potential through creativity, independence, spontaneity, and a grasp of the real world. In learning about self-actualization we can fully comprehend what skill sets are and how discovering your true potential will assist you with positive growth. Skills are passions, talents, and abilities that sometimes become concealed. We tend to focus on areas that lie on the surface, but once you discover other areas of interest it opens channels in your decision-making process.

Now that you can make effective decisions and rid yourself of fear, you will be able to set and reach goals . . .

Goals: Eliminate Your Saboteurs

Everyone needs a personal and professional goal—long term and short term. People without goals are lost. For the goal-setting process to be successful we need to be able to identify our saboteurs—our fears—or what is blocking us from reaching our desired outcome. You must understand where your limitations stem from. Identifying that is foremost, and then you can move forward toward the implementation of your plan.

Many steps need to be implemented in the goal process. First of all, you need to identify the ending result and act as if you've already achieved that success. You need to understand the conscious and subconscious mind and how they can propel you to greater heights or limit you from reaching your goals.

I will educate you on the importance of positive affirmations and auto-suggestion, which will bypass many negatives and accelerate positive change. Being able to visualize the end result will place it on the screen of your mind and enhance creative imagination. Look at the successful men and women in history and how they began by visualizing what they wanted to accomplish.

To successfully visualize your goal, you must be able to understand relaxation and why it is imperative to use your senses. This will determine your mindset, and the successful person does not live in a competitive mindset but rather a creative one. There is no room for competitiveness; it will only create additional worry, fear, and doubt, which will cripple you.

Once you fully comprehend the importance of the goal-setting process you will create SMART goals: Specific, Measurable, Attainable, Realistic, and Timely. I've discussed the saboteurs that limit us from reaching our desired outcome. Those saboteurs come from our multitude of habits, which is our paradigm.

How do we change our paradigm, and how does that create positive corporate paradigms . . . ?

A Healthy Corporate Paradigm

Just as your personal paradigm is your multitude of habits, your corporate paradigm is a multitude of habits as a group. This is commonly known as corporate culture— your workplace habits. A habit is an idea fixed within your subconscious mind that causes you to produce actions without any conscious thought. I will help you understand that your conscious mind is your reasoning mind, and once you accept a thought at the conscious level, it then goes into the subconscious mind, and that is what produces your actions. Your actions become habitual, and this can produce positive or negative results.

At times we do things we do not want to do and get results we do not want, but we do it anyway. For someone to experience permanent change, whether personally or professionally, there must be a change in the primary cause of their results. We can make these changes when we fully comprehend the power of the mind. These habits that we discover took place in the developmental periods of our childhood, and I will discuss the importance of understanding that timeline.

Our paradigm creates our self-image, which also has an impact on our perception. Our perception stems from implementation of thought, combined with utilizing our senses, thus producing habits. That process can cause fear, worry, and doubt—all of which need to be eliminated.

Eliminating this negative process can only be done once we back it with faith.

How does the application of faith and intuition move us to the next level of eliminating the terror barrier . . . ?

Burn The Boats—Conquer Your Fears

The ancient Greek warriors were both feared and respected by their enemies for their reputation of unsurpassed bravery and commitment to victory. Once the warriors arrived on the enemy's shore, the commanders ordered them to "burn the boats." With no boats to retreat to, the army had to be successful in order to survive. As the soldiers watched the boats burn, they realized there was no turning back—no surrendering. The same stands true in your own life and where you have arrived. That is why I love that story—you have no excuses for failure. You MUST "win" or perish.

The meaning behind burning the boats is being able to trust and have faith so that you are able to conquer your fears. You will acquire a deep motivation that will allow you to propel yourself to new heights. You'll feel as though you are able to conquer anything that stands in your way of prevailing. You WILL reach your desired outcome.

To obtain a level of faith you must learn how to identify and then implement your "mental muscles." Once you discover how to apply them you will attain a level of desire that allows you to utilize your power of will. The mental faculties you will learn allow your inner strength to propel you forward.

Eliminate that fear, back it with faith, and make that revolutionary change . . .

Revolutionary Change

What does a revolutionary change mean?

It is a jump to exponential growth, whereas incremental steps provide slight growth with precautionary measures. To take that leap you will have acquired faith and allowed your intuition to guide you. It is being able to recognize what has been planted in your subconscious mind and your limitless capabilities. It is not about taking unnecessary risks but rather knowing that you can take your position to a level where you can grow with no fear. It provides excitement, which generates vibration and maintains a positive energy flow. This is where the law of attraction/vibration generates success. It puts you in tune with your senses, and you begin to attract people and circumstances to help you reach your desired outcome.

You will become highly motivated and your attitude will reflect positivity. An attitude of gratitude will provide you with a sense of appreciation. You need to be grateful for all the good in your life. Once you have implemented all the aforementioned success principles, you will confidently network with likeminded individuals.

You will combine your knowledge, experience, and spirit of harmony to serve one another through a group; you will mastermind . . .

Mastermind For Success

Masterminding is the coordination of knowledge and effort, in a spirit of harmony, between two or more people for the attainment of a definite purpose. This will be your mastermind team. I will teach you how to implement a group, conduct the meeting, and discover the benefits of placing likeminded individuals in a setting that will produce positive results. You will achieve your desired outcome.

You will challenge each other to create and implement goals and hold each other accountable. This group will allow you to brainstorm ideas and provide support backed with total honesty. Networking together promotes growth and expansion in your business and personal career. It will create energy and enhance interpersonal relations by supporting each other. The meeting of minds is an extension of your intelligence and will be a reference point of expectations.

Think of it as having your own objective board of directors that will continually move you forward in personal and professional growth.

RELAX—GROW—FIND SUCCESS AND HAPPINESS . . .

Fuel Your Growth With Zero-Gravity Relaxation

By the time you reach this chapter you will:

- Become a better person—turn negativity to positivity
- Eliminate worry, fear, and doubt and replace them with positivity
- Set and reach goals
- Become motivated and persistent, develop your intuition, and then back it with faith
- Find balance between career and family obligations
- Make sound business decisions
- Understand the conscious and subconscious mind, create a positive corporate paradigm, and then make a quantum leap

- Build your own networking group (mastermind)
- Become a valued leader!

Now implement the aforementioned principles with relaxation—zero gravity. Zero gravity is weightlessness, or an absence of weight. This creates an absence of stress and strain resulting from externally applied mechanical contact forces.

Understand the importance of meditation and relaxation then allow the zero gravity experience to help you. Zero gravity is sensory deprivation, the deliberate reduction or removal of stimuli from one or more of the senses.

How does it help you?

The zero gravity experience helps you physically and spiritually and enhances learning and creativity. It helps with pain at all levels, sports, concentration, etc. This is an exciting chapter to help you understand all the health and mind benefits.

What is the zero gravity experience?

It is floating in a pool filled with Epsom salt. Learn the benefits of combining Epsom salt with the zero gravity experience. Epsom salt is magnesium sulfate, which has many health benefits (i.e. relaxation, relieves pain and cramping, regulates fluid retention in cells, facilitates the body's use of calcium to transmit chemical signals throughout the nervous system, improves circulation to prevent serious cardiovascular illness by decreasing inflammation and protecting the elasticity of arteries, regulates blood sugar, soothes sprains, exfoliates your skin, and much more). This is a very interesting chapter of learning how to take your mind and body to a totally different level.

Relax . . . float . . . enjoy.
REVOLUTIONIZE YOUR CORPORATE LIFE!

Chapter 1
Maximize Your Leadership

A leader is one who knows the way, goes the way, and shows the way.

—John Maxwell

People ask the difference between a leader and a boss. The leader leads, and the boss drives.

—Theodore Roosevelt

Most of our organizational habits and routines reflect the behaviors of earlier leaders. A good leader has the ability to inspire others and assist them with setting and reaching goals. Leadership is the foundation of success. Leaders can't be defined as born or bred. I believe that all humans have the ability to exhibit leadership. Although some may be born with these abilities, they need to be nurtured and developed. If we focused on instilling these skills in our children we would see a new generation of leaders and entrepreneurs. Anyone can be a leader.

You must also realize the important role leadership plays on a personal level. Everything you learn in this chapter should help you on a personal level and allow you to comprehend how leadership can affect your family. Every leader needs to be compassionate, resolute, well rounded, and patient. Along with those traits, it is imperative to have the ability to manage diverse personalities and skills toward a common goal or mission. Once you've achieved those goals you will have garnered the respect of those you are leading.

Many individuals do not understand that experiencing failure can make you a successful leader, but those experiences actually help to create a well-disciplined, focused, and empathetic leader. As with many aspects of life and business, communication and self-awareness enhance your leadership skills. Most great leaders began in the capacity of intelligent followers. When they receive a suggestion from a follower that has merit, they quickly investigate the idea. When they determine the other person's idea is superior to their own, they reject their own idea, accept the other person's idea, and work with it as if it were their own. They will also publicly give the person who originated the idea full credit. They do not have an ego problem or a competitive mindset, but rather a creative plane. An effective leader is truly a creative visionary and active listener.

Leaders should expect discomfort and inconsistency as their employees begin to change behavior. A leader should have:

- Vision
- Understanding of creative abilities
- Ability to create anything individually
- Great attitude, which is a composite of thoughts, feelings, and actions
- Passion
- Motivation
- Effective communication
- Ability to offer rewards and recognition
- Creativity and desire for new things
- Clarity of direction
- Respect and responsibility
- Courage and willingness to change
- Self-control
- Keen sense of justice
- Decisions
- Pleasant personality
- Sympathy and understanding
- Mastery of detail
- Willingness to assume full responsibility
- Cooperation

So how do you acquire those attributes?

Leadership is a social dynamic. One key factor in becoming an effective leader is having the ability to combine entrepreneurial skills with emotion. A good leader works toward assisting his/her team with goals. I continually discuss the importance of goals. In order to set and reach goals you must acquire the ability to become motivated. Motivation is a leadership quality. It is the driving force behind all of an individual's actions. There are different forms of motivation including intrinsic, extrinsic, physiological, and achievement. Intrinsic sources include physical, mental, emotional, and spiritual. Extrinsic sources include operant and social conditioning. Some examples of needs within these categories are:

- Physical—avoidance of pain, hunger, fatigue, etc.
- Mental—cognitive behavior, developing interest, and problem solving
- Spiritual—understanding the purpose of one's life and connecting one's life to deeper meanings
- Achievement—reaching success and achieving one's aspirations in life

Self-motivated people know there is no simple solution to becoming motivated after a disappointment, but they also know they can overcome adversity, and they are stronger when faced with challenges. Self-motivated individuals realize their thoughts control their emotions. They learn how to elevate their thoughts to create a positive outcome, which helps them remain focused on long-term goals and not the temporary, less desirable situation.

Motivated people are generally happier and more energetic, and they see positive results in their minds. Some people have learned how motivation will improve their life, and they create a vision that is realistic as well as an approach to seek new challenges and methods to grow. It is an inspiration that is continual. Lack of motivation produces no results or brings only mediocre results, whereas motivation brings quicker, better, and greater results.

There is a lot more to leadership than having the ability to lead other people. True leadership is about team building and leveraging your team's strengths to reach the desired outcome. You not only have to be able to see the obstacles, but you must envision the solution.

As a leader you need to communicate in a way that makes people believe in you and know they can count on you for support. You never lose sight of the mission or what you are trying to achieve. In the following chapters I discuss many principles, and it is your job as a leader to help implement them. Take for instance the chapter on goals and the quantum leap. They go hand-in-hand. You want your team to have big goals and learn how to conquer the fear of failure.

You must keep up morale, which is the mental, emotional, and spiritual state of a person. You also must fully understand the dynamics of your team and how to handle the negative individuals. To do this, first you must identify people in the organization that cause conflict and negativity.

The following is a list of negative personalities:

- Pessimists: they expect the worst-case scenario and can cause a huge decrease in morale.
- Angry temperament: they have an explosive personality and often get angry at the slightest provocation.
- Complainers: they present negative scenarios explaining how everything is wrong and will go wrong.
- Self-absorbed: they constantly seek credit.
- Bypassers: they bypass superiors and take over.
- Procrastinators: they keep putting things off, which can cause delay in project completions.
- Resisters: they resist change.
- Moody: they shift their moods and expect others to adjust to them. This also causes a decrease in morale.
- Blamers: they blame everyone else instead of taking responsibility for their own setbacks or mistakes.
- Victims: they believe people are out to get them and can't let go of things in the past that went wrong.

You need to be able to identify problematic areas and personalities for a positive team-building experience. In that particular identification process, it is key for you to understand a person's representational system. What does that mean? A representational system is the way the person represents the world. Two people can enter a room and describe the experience completely differently. Understanding this system will also help you communicate more effectively. You will pay attention and begin to talk the same language. The three primary representational systems are:

1. Visual: A visual person references conversations based upon what they see. They usually speak quickly, are highly motivated, and tend to switch from one subject to another rapidly. This type of individual leaves out small details and focuses on the main part of the conversation. A visual person takes action immediately and is able to multitask effectively.

2. Auditory: An auditory person references conversations based upon what they hear. They are generally calm and tend to "go with the flow."

3. Kinesthetic: A kinesthetic person references conversations based upon feelings. They speak slowly and are detail oriented. They give details while telling a story and think before they speak. They also think before they act upon a situation.

Understanding the representational system will decrease stress in a leadership role because you will be able to communicate the needs of the company effectively. It will also aid in personal relationships.

So, what improvements do you make to create an effective leadership and team-building model?

- Take the negative conflict and fuel it with positive passion. Conflict and debate can be healthy. When people debate situations, whether positive or negative, it is still interaction and communication, which is good. Opposition can be beneficial, and it can allow for preventative measures.

- Look for any negative self-talk and find a way to counter it with positive. As a leader you need to implement the complete opposite of what is being displayed as negative—that is your positive. Take the presenting challenges and collaborate as a group to find the solutions that will move your team forward.

- Find the right employees. Look for the optimists instead of the pessimists. You will be able to empower them to make innovative changes.

- Create a relaxing and positive environment. Help the more negative personalities to implement the non-serious side of things.

- Spend time and energy to inspire those who are negative. Find ways to give them credit and take responsibility for some of their mistakes. Suspend your judgment and have humility. This will show fairness, and you will be rewarded with loyalty and dedication.

- Incorporate creativity and you will find that you are able to lead the followers in a new direction.

- Maintain a calm and confident manner. No matter how difficult the situation, you must remain in control. This allows you to assess the situation and make sound decisions.

- Always take action and address every situation. Determine what went wrong, and use your analysis to correct it. Develop a strategic plan of action. Build solidarity within the organization.

While making positive improvements, think about the law of relativity: nothing is big or small, fast or slow, good or bad until you relate it to something else. Everything just "is." Don't relate your results to another's success. Instead, relate it to what you are truly trying to accomplish.

In my education and mentorship, I have learned a daily six-point program for creating an image of leadership. I implemented it far before it was presented to me; however, writing it down in chronological order will help you keep it in the front of your mind.

1. RELAX:
   Throughout this book I discuss the importance of relaxation because relaxation renews and tension tires. Leaders are highly results-oriented and able to multitask productively. Creative energy flows freely through the mind and body when relaxed. Yoga and meditation are key to relaxation.

2. CHANGE:
   If what you are currently doing is not working, form new habits for essential growth. There are many areas we must continually review for change:
   • Personal appearance
   • Personal life
   • Social life
   • Personal development program

- Health
- Work habits
- Attitude
- Time and stress management
- Work and personal balance
- Business associates

3. EDUCATE:

   Continually educate yourself by watching and listening to positive video and audio programs. Listening to them and then verbalizing positive affirmations will allow you to reach your desired outcome. Once you know them you will be able to implement the repetitive process so that you can accelerate change.

4. LISTEN:

   I also discuss the art of listening multiple times throughout this book. Listening is a great tool for all leaders. Listen to positive audios in your car instead of music, news, and sports. Also, master the art of listening to others. We tend to get caught up with controlling conversation; however, you can learn a lot by just listening. You will be able to determine personality types, strengths, weaknesses, and self-image.

5. COMMUNICATE:

   This is most important because it allows you to understand your employees, clients, and personal acquaintances. I recommend modeling the behavior of other successful businesspeople. Create your own network of people.

Also, learn how to communicate with others by understanding their behavior. That is why watching and listening to others is so important.

6. AWARENESS:

Self-awareness is critical, and you must also be able to promote self-awareness with the individuals you deal with on a daily basis. Understanding your inner core as well as others' will help you discover how changes will benefit everyone. It will also help you carry out a strategic plan of action so you will reach your desired outcome. Awareness helps you determine what you are doing well, what needs to be repaired, and then how to make positive changes. The more you enhance the recognition of self-awareness, the better your understanding of how to eliminate saboteurs.

There are seven levels of awareness:

1. Animalistic—this state is how we react, our fight-or-flight response. This describes one who responds by stopping and thinking and then thinking and acting.

2. Mass consciousness—this state is derived from habit and controlled by others. However, it can also be independent. It teaches us to go in the opposite direction of everyone else and break out! Earl Nightingale talked about crowds of people moving in the same direction, with a few people going the opposite direction. He said if you followed the few people going in the opposite direction you'd probably never make another mistake.

3. Aspiring—this state is a constant reach to be more and have more. Something within you wants to live a fuller life. (Be more, do more, have more.)

4. Individual consciousness—this state allows us to express our uniqueness as a human being. Don't worry about what others think.

5. Discipline—this state gives you a command, and by following that command you will enhance your willpower.

6. Educate—this describes learning so you can discipline yourself. When you continually educate yourself you will increase your power of positivity.

7. Master—in this state you master what you're doing and stop letting the physical world control you. Instead, control yourself. Let your thoughts guide your world.

Most people begin with their present results:

Thoughts + feelings + action = same results. If you change your present outcome you must begin by changing your thoughts.

Find ways to keep the lines of communication open. Remember:

COMMUNICATION IS KEY!

Within the executive arena I find that the most effective tool is calmness and motivation, which go together. This is the beginning step to being able to apply the responsibilities of the job. If you are not calm and motivated, you will not produce positive results. What causes an individual to be hurried, anxious, or a procrastinator? Better yet, how do you fix it?

By managing time and stress! Once you understand this and work on repairing it, you are on the path to success.

Chapter 2
Manage Your Time And Stress—
Not The Other Way Around

Time is the most valuable coin in your life. You and you alone will determine how that coin will be spent. Be careful that you do not let other people spend it for you.
—Carl Sandburg

He who every morning plans the transactions of that day and follows that plan carries a thread that will guide him through the labyrinth of the most busy life.
—Victor Hugo

D id you ever attempt to get to work early and everything goes wrong: car won't start, you can't get in touch with the mechanic, your furnace isn't working properly, etc. The clock continually ticks … time is running out … you begin to panic. Sound familiar? Each of us has experienced those things at one time or another.

You must first learn how to declutter your mind. You will never be able to remain calm in stressful situations if you don't know how to quiet your mind. Throughout this book I discuss the importance of relaxation/meditation. Meditation is greatly misunderstood. There is no right or wrong way to meditate. I can give many examples of how to begin, but it takes months of practice before you start to see the positive impact. You will definitely become more productive in the workplace. So many of my business clients are astounded by the benefits of meditation. In suggesting it to many individuals they are sometimes at first reluctant; however, once they learn it they attest that they are far more focused and accomplished.

Some examples of ways to meditate:

- Listen to inspirational music
- Listen to guided meditation, which is inspirational music combined with words
- Lie or sit in total silence

The objective is not only to quiet the mind, but to clear it. Rid yourself of internal chatter.

Think of it in the physical exercise realm. When we exercise we strengthen muscles and tone our bodies. Well, meditation works the same way, only we're strengthening the mind. Being calm and strong in your mind will produce productivity and better decision making, and it will allow you to turn negative situations into positive ones. Once you learn how to meditate, schedule ten minutes a day to practice it. Meditation is a positive interruption, and trust me—you will be more productive. If you are unable to declutter your mind, time and stress management issues will increase over time.

A wise goal for those in a corporate setting is to utilize time more efficiently. One of the biggest complaints I hear is that there are too many emails and not enough time to continually check them. Check your emails twice a day. Begin in the morning, preferably after meditation. If you get up earlier to allow time for meditating, you can check your emails before you leave the house. This will give you a work-time advantage.

Sort mail by categorizing:

- Read now
- Handle now
- Read later

To create that additional time in the morning, prepare for your day the night before. Once you are in the routine of getting up early you will find yourself wanting to go into the office. Most people are more productive in the morning, so go to the office before others arrive. This will increase productivity because you will have quiet time in which to get more accomplished. Utilize your time driving to work to continue the calmness in your mind. Instead of listening to the negativity of the news, you can listen to something positive or use the time to repeat positive affirmations.

Once you are at the office there are many areas in which you can implement additional procedures that will assist you with time. For example, utilize technology by setting up reminders, paying bills online, and using it to get organized. This will help to reduce things that waste time. Also, start setting appointments with yourself. We tend to keep work appointments, so make your personal ones just as important. You should actually plan your personal time on the calendar before your work time. This habit will have an impact on your mind as a reminder that you and your family come first, or better yet, YOU come first.

Many people say that while they are making great progress at work, interruptions begin with phone calls and colleagues. It is so easy to get in the habit of listening to the negativity of others. Instead of accepting every phone call, set aside time to allow calls to be forwarded to a message center, or have someone screen your calls to eliminate the ones that are time wasters. As for the colleagues and conversation interruptions, place a Do Not Disturb sign on your door until you have completed your project. It does not mean that you do not care about your colleagues or their family, but if your goal is to create additional time then you must eliminate areas that take away from work projects.

You can also learn to delegate the smaller things. Build yourself a support network personally and professionally. Choose those individuals who can eliminate some of your smaller tasks. Find a way to include family members on home projects and errands, or hire someone to help you with them.

This will help you establish priorities and realistically analyze your time. Learn the difference between where you can help and where you are needed. Most importantly, do not be afraid to ask for help. Also, analyze the difference between needing it now and needing it at all.

Good organizational skills will help you with time and stress. Create "to do" lists, and mark items off as you complete them. Categorize them relative to A, B, and C—A should be priority, B is in the middle, and C is least important. Many people do a to-do list and lump it all into one list. Should you go in that direction, your list will just grow and you will become overwhelmed. Categorizing it assists with mind control. Once you achieve positive results in accomplishing the most important tasks first, you will become motivated and your B and C list will be very easy. Also, keep your office organized. Remember, there is a place for everything and everything in its place.

Once you begin to make progress it will be easier to set boundaries and learn to say no to colleagues. Boundaries and limits help you take charge of your time and feelings. Do not allow anything to interfere with things you have scheduled with your family. We all realize how important goal setting is. We continually strive to meet our professional goals. However, don't forget about the importance of personal and family goals. Setting family goals will aid in time management. With goals you need accountability. Ensure that you choose a good accountability partner because most people tend to procrastinate. It really needs to be someone who is willing to tell you things you may not want to hear. They need to be firm with you, but also fair. They have to have the ability to distinguish time wasters. At times an accountability partner will allow you to let things slide in certain scenarios; however, their main objective is to help you reach your desired outcome.

One major problem with goal setting is that many people tend to procrastinate. Procrastination will prohibit you from reaching goals, so replace it with persistence. Persistence is an essential factor in the process of transmuting desire into its monetary equivalent. There is no substitute for persistence. If you do not learn how to become persistent you will not achieve success. To become persistent, you must first know what you want. A strong motive forces one to surmount many difficulties. You must have the desire to pursue the object of your intensity. This will develop your self-reliance and help you formulate organized plans for the development of your goal.

The basis of persistence is the power of will. Napoleon Hill's book *Think and Grow Rich* discusses the importance of persistence. He states, "Will-power and desire, when properly combined make an irresistible pair. Those who accumulate great fortunes are generally known as cold-blooded, and sometimes ruthless. Often they are misunderstood. What they have is will-power, which they mix with persistence, and place it in back of their desires to insure the attainment of their objectives.

How do you know if you lack persistence?

- Failure to recognize and clearly define exactly what you want
- Procrastination
- Lack of interest in acquiring a team of people who work together in a spirit of harmony

- Indecisiveness
- Creating alibis/excuses
- Lack of interest
- Blaming others
- Quit at first sign of defeat/failure
- Lack of goals
- Inability to develop intuition
- Wishing instead of willing
- Compromising poverty instead of creating wealth
- Trying to get without giving
- Fear of criticism & poverty

When you are setting goals be sure to create time for yourself. You are no good to family or colleagues if you can't find time to relax, relieve tension, and minimize stress. Family is most important; however, we tend to put our professions first.

Why?

Because many people realize that family is the most understanding and accommodating. Begin to enhance your communication skills with your spouse. Messages of disappointment within family many times go unnoticed due to lack of communication. Include your family in as many areas as you can. Put together an exercise program that includes everyone. This gives everyone a sense of accomplishment while creating that special bonding time. One area that many people fall short with is dinnertime. That is also bonding time, and many families do not implement good dinner habits. Recognize that dinner is key communication time. Do not allow electronics at the table, listen to your spouse and children when they talk, but most importantly, contribute to the conversation. Discuss the positives of the day and turn the negatives around. The negatives can be used as productive time to problem solve the situation. Every problem has a solution.

Allowing yourself that extra time in the morning and implementing the organizational skills I previously mentioned will allow you to manage your time and stress effectively. Your day will be structured in a calm and positive way, you will accomplish your tasks in a timelier fashion, and you will therefore have time to spend with your family. Spending additional time with your family needs to be stress and worry free. If you are spending time with family and your mind remains at work, there will be no benefit. So get yourself excited and begin managing your time.

So, what is stress and how do we manage it? We touched on this earlier, but it bears repeating in this chapter on time and stress management.

Stress is any physical, chemical, or emotional reaction to the ever increasing demands of life that cause bodily or mental unrest. Managing your stress level will increase your ability to cope with life's challenges.

The following are signs of poor stress/time management:

- Irritability—Do you feel yourself being short with family, friends, and co-workers?
- Fatigue—Are you tired during the day or when you arrive at home?
- Difficulty concentrating—Is your mind wandering and you are unable to focus?

- Being absentminded—Do you continually forget where you place things or forget what your daily agenda is?
- Loss of sleep—Do you find yourself tossing and turning or waking in the middle of the night and are unable to go back to sleep?
- Physical disorders—Are you challenged in any physical arena?
- Becoming withdrawn—Do you find yourself desiring to be alone or unable to make conversation in social settings?
- Depression—Are you continually sad or just feeling as though you aren't happy enough?

In addition to the aforementioned suggestions on organizational structure, the following is a list of techniques to manage stress:

- Talk to a professional. It is okay to seek outside consultation with anyone who has a therapeutic background. Sometimes you need an outsider to heighten your awareness on your present situation and advise positive alternatives. It does not mean that you should seek counsel from a psychologist or psychiatrist. You can consult with an executive coach, who will provide a strategic plan of action to assist you in reaching your desired outcome.
- Heighten your awareness to muscle tension. When you experience anxiety it is not uncommon for your

body to become tight. You need to practice relaxation techniques. Once you recognize the outward symptoms you will be able to structure yourself inwardly.

- Delegate. Implement procedures that will allow you to sort your responsibilities, and delegate the least important to those who have extra time to accept those projects.

- Get an accountability partner to keep you on track. Ask someone who is willing to be firm and fair on a daily basis relative to your needs.

- Do something that makes you feel good. There is nothing better than feeling good about yourself. It is a necessity.

- Have a "me" day—laugh and have fun. You will be more productive once you are happy within yourself.

- Write weekly status reports. This allows you to track your progress. It assists you in discovering Productive Actions (PA) vs. Non-Productive Actions (NPA).

- Do additional planning, problem solving, and decision making.

- Keep yourself organized. Once you organize everything you will become additionally motivated.

- Get physical exercise. This provides a sense of self-worth and is also a great motivator. Feeling good on the outside makes you feel better on the inside.

- Take advantage of your down time. This is a time when you can appreciate relaxation and regain focus on your schedule.

Stress can cause many problems in many areas, so recognizing symptoms is the first step. I have personally mastered the steps in eliminating stress and managing time, and I believe it is the key component to success on a personal and professional level. Once you understand it and learn how to eliminate it, you can effectively learn how to balance your career and family obligations. They work hand-in-hand and will bring you contentment at both levels.

So, how do we find that balance?

Chapter 3

Hand-In-Hand: Balancing
Your Career And Family

Life is like riding a bicycle. To keep your balance, you must keep moving.

—Albert Einstein

Happiness is not a matter of intensity but of balance, order, rhythm and harmony.

—Thomas Merton

W hether a client comes to me for personal development or executive coaching, there is one area that applies to both and that is balancing career and family. This is a very big issue. It's difficult to leave work at work and home at home. The smallest changes can produce the strongest impacts.

There are four keys to transformation that I want to share with you here. Whether business or personal, the starting-point issue is that you don't know what you want, and once you discover it, you are unaware of how to get there.

1. Key #1: Time and Stress Management
   Focus on one project at a time. I previously stated many key points relative to time and stress management. Understanding the four keys to transformation listed here will assist you with balancing career and family.

2. Key #2: Personal Growth/Self-awareness
   Vision your future, write it down, and begin to take action. Look for deep connection and meaning in the relationship you have with yourself, your family, your day-to-day experiences, your spouse, and your higher self. Tune into your life and live in the moment. Also, reward yourself.

3. Key #3: Balance
   Finding that balance with career and family obligations. In coaching I have discovered that balance is key in all aspects of life.

4. Key #4: Earning Money and Giving Back
   Look for ways to give your time, services, goods, or resources to a noteworthy cause. This will give you a strong sense of purpose. You can't do good deeds without money; therefore, it is not a negative

to have the desire for it as long as your intentions are good.

Once you understand the four keys to transformation you can focus on balance.

Where do you begin?

I've mentioned the power of meditation and gratitude over and over throughout the chapters of this book. Why? Because gratitude is the most powerful and most people don't even consider it. Gratitude is something we all take for granted. Morning gratitude helps with self-reflection on the importance of family and life. Learning to be grateful places you in a positive energy flow and helps to eliminate negativity throughout your day. Science dictates that we are energy. It is imperative to get yourself flowing with positive energy, especially in the morning.

William James said the greatest discovery of his generation was that you could alter your life by altering your attitude of mind.

Attitude Is Everything!

Your attitude controls what happens to you, and vibrations (negative or positive) dictate what you will attract.

Gaining that calmness at the beginning of your day puts family obligations into perspective. Morning exercise will also aid in a positive start to your day. I previously stated that exercise is an internal motivator. Once you are calm you can do many things to internalize on the happiness of your family. Look at family pictures in the morning and several times throughout the day. It will help to remind you of the importance of staying balanced. It also gives you something to look forward to when you are frustrated at work and long to be with those you love.

One mistake people make is getting caught up in phone calls. In the previous chapter I discussed how to handle phone calls from a corporate level, but what about those personal calls from home. This can be a positive or a negative so limit yourself to one call each day. Even if it is a positive call, you could wait until you arrive at home. That phone call takes up valuable time. And in the case that it ends negatively, it will cause you to redirect your focus from the task at hand. Limiting your calls will actually aid in strengthening your relationship(s) because it prohibits any negative situation. When we experience a negative phone call we tend to stay stuck in it throughout the day because there isn't adequate time for resolution.

In addition to that, there are many ways to keep your relationship strong and healthy. For instance, remember this: it takes one minute per day to make a relationship successful. A kind word or act can be done in that one minute or less and creates a positive start. Learning balance from a personal level will help you with it professionally.

Again, remember the importance of effective communication. Clearly discuss your family obligations with your superior. This allows you to establish a plan of action with your boss and will prevent you from feeling overwhelmed and strained between the two. It will also help your boss to understand your level of priority, especially if you have a special-needs child, new parenting responsibilities, educational requirements, or multiple sports obligations. These are all areas that require additional levels of commitment. As you learn this professional balance keep track of everything.

A key idea to assist in multiple areas is to keep a journal. I suggest you have two separate ones—one relative to work and one for personal use. This is very important and will help you track your progress. It is important to track your ability to eliminate negatives, and journaling will gauge the length of time you stay stuck in it. It will also allow you to keep track of your PA (productive actions) and NPA (non-productive actions). Eliminating time wasters will alleviate stress.

Time and stress management play a major role in finding ways to balance career and family. They go hand-in-hand. For example: after-work socializing can interfere with your personal life, but there are times it is a necessity in your career. Find ways to balance those after-work socialization functions successfully. It is difficult and stressful to try to participate in multiple events, so prioritize them relative to importance. Also, if your spouse is a stay-at-home spouse you need to think about their needs. That spouse is probably looking forward to good conversation and quality relationship time. If you can include them in the after-work socialization functions, it creates a way for the two of you to spend quality time together and still meet your corporate needs.

On your way home from the office try to unwind. In the aforementioned chapters I discussed the importance of using your time driving to work. It is equally important for the drive home. Use this time to minimize your stress and eliminate the negativity from your day. If you take negativity home with you it will create additional stress within the family. Once you arrive at home engage yourself with family. Again, eat dinner together and turn off cell phones and TV so that you can be engaged in family discussions about their day. Do not discuss your negativity from work, and when they mention a negative occurrence, attempt to turn it around. Be in the moment.

Young people who are new in careers and starting a family tend to pick up habits from childhood, so learn how to utilize these steps to balance both. This will make you more successful.

If you are a working mom, lose the guilt. Numerous articles discuss the fact that infants who grow up with working mothers are well adjusted. As with anything there are pros and cons to either side of it, and let's face it, sometimes working mothers need assistance.

There are benefits to having a caregiver, such as:

- Eliminates nervousness
- Causes less parental dependency
- Provides a sense of trust, self-soothing, flexibility, and better socialization skills. Having good socialization skills in itself has many benefits. It definitely enhances friendships, creates effective communication, and provides interpersonal relations.

Having a caregiver can be extremely beneficial; however, other factors also play into your children's behavior and moods. For example, ensure that they are getting the proper amount of sleep. Take proactive steps to getting them to sleep longer stretches. They should have between six and eight hours of sleep every night. In my coaching experience I see a pattern of teenagers who are allowed to stay up late on the computer, doing homework, watching movies, or playing video games. This will affect the educational process along with mood swings.

If your child is involved in sports activities adjust your expectations. Do not allow your children to reschedule practices or games unless it is an absolute necessity. Many parents feel that the more their kids are involved in, the less trouble they will encounter. I disagree with that. Getting your children involved in too many activities becomes overwhelming for everyone. It can clutter your ability to serve both roles. However, I equally feel it is important to make them finish what they start. If they do decide to be in a sport and then want to quit, you are allowing them to have a negative impact on the team. Team building is a great quality to teach your children because they will carry it into adulthood. Part of leadership is team building. It isn't solely about you as an individual, but how your behavior impacts your team.

Once you are able to balance career and family obligations, you and your children will be less stressed. This helps to create a positive marriage as well and opens up additional "me time," which is something we all need. That balance coupled with time and stress management will create a positive environment and healthy relationships. Once you understand the role of the leader and eliminate time wasters, negativity, and stress you will be able to make better decisions. People take the decision-making process for granted, but it is of the utmost importance in every aspect of our lives.

Chapter 4
The Decisive Leader

Decide what you want. Decide what you are prepared to give up to get it. Set your mind on it. Get on with the work.

—H.L. Hunt

Any thought that is passed on to the subconscious often enough and convincingly enough is finally accepted.

—Robert Collier

Why are decisions an important part of your business?

One of the greatest skills a leader can have is the ability to make effective business decisions. There are many benefits to business leaders who are decisive. A decisive leader has a major impact on the success of the company. It starts by influencing morale because employees respect management when they make decisions. Whenever I bring up the word "decisions" people tend to take it for granted, but keep in mind that many influential factors go into the process of decision making. It is a combination of education, intuition, skills, and experience. You may ask yourself, why trust intuition on something that will have such an impact on the business? However, once you learn how to truly develop your intuition, you will grow to trust it and be able to make quick decisions.

The information in this chapter is not just about decisions being made by the owner of the company. It can be applicable in any managerial position or of great benefit to the laborer who desires to make a career change or the individual who is entertaining thoughts of starting a business.

For example:

Clients who come to me for help in starting their own entrepreneurial venture also have to make the decision based upon their personal situation. The very first step before you can develop your plan is to analyze the effect it will have on those around you. What do you hope to accomplish? Why do you want to venture out into the entrepreneurial world? If it were easy everyone would do it. My goal in writing this book is to help you analyze every situation to either assist you in a new venture or excel your existing position to new heights.

People tend to become indecisive rather than making a decision due to fear of making the wrong choice. They think "What if . . . ?" Be very cautious of the "what if" statement because being indecisive creates fear, worry, and doubt, which can become very crippling. Many people continually focus on things that may never happen.

Napoleon Hill's book *Think and Grow Rich* discusses the accurate analysis of over twenty-five thousand men and women who had experienced failure. This analysis disclosed the fact that lack of decision was near the head of the list of the thirty major causes of failure. This is no mere statement of a theory; it is a fact. Procrastination is the opposite of decision and is a common enemy that practically every man or woman must conquer.

Opportunity never sneaks up on those who straddle the fence of indecision. Indecision wastes time that could be spent on more productive tasks. Successful people avoid unnecessary risks by implementing their decisions after careful consideration. Making a decision has the potential to improve almost any personal or business situation you will ever encounter, and it could literally propel you down the path to incredible success.

So how can you be sure you're making the best decision to lead you to success?

When opportunities surface you need to take the steps toward the decision-making process:

- Identify the problem
- Analyze it and gather the necessary information and resources
- Make a list of the pros and cons
- Internally evaluate it using education, skills, experience, and intuition

- Follow through
- Create a strategic plan of action
- Monitor your progress and make changes if you need to
- Most importantly—MAKE A DECISION!

Now that you've made a decision, be clear on the objective.

One of Henry Ford's most outstanding qualities was his habit of reaching decisions quickly and definitely, and changing them slowly. It was this quality that prompted him to continue manufacturing his famous Model T when all of his advisors, and many of the purchasers of the car, were urging him to change it. Do not allow yourself to be influenced by others.

A personal example of not allowing the opinion of others is when I decided to open an executive and personal development coaching business. Everyone's opinion was the unlikeliness of being able to bring coaching to a small town. The majority response was, "It's for the cities." I disagreed. I did not allow those opinions to interfere with my business decision. I could personally see the benefit and knew it was an extremely rewarding career to be able to propel people to new heights, both personally and professionally. It's about saving lives and helping others set and reach their goals.

Recognition of your strengths and weaknesses will help keep you out of harm's way. Being able to recognize a good decision makes the process easy; however, ones that are more complicated require more reflection. Whether personally or professionally, it is imperative to learn "calmness of mind" and how important it is. Bringing order to your mind allows you to make better decisions, and those who can do that without the influence of others are the same people who become successful leaders in business.

It took me a very long time to fully comprehend the importance and impact decisions make on your life. Many decisions are driven by fear, which isn't real. Fear is something that you create in your mind. Instead of allowing fear to create obstacles, analyze the steps I previously discussed, and remember you must do it with a clear mind.

The person who fails to develop their ability to make decisions is destined to fail because indecision sets up internal conflicts that can create a tug-of-war in your mind. Indecision is the seedling of fear, indecision crystallizes into doubt, and the two blended together become fear—fear being the most crippling. Low self-esteem or lack of self-confidence is the real culprit. Decision makers are not afraid of failure. They know they can learn from their negative experiences; therefore they will never submit to the failure. They also have a very strong self-image and a high degree of self-esteem.

Bob Proctor has been an invaluable mentor to me. He is a very successful businessman and wise leader. When I first met him and he discussed the importance of the decision-making process, I found myself giving careful consideration to every step of my business. He talked about when John Kennedy asked Wernher von Braun what it would take to build a rocket that would carry a man to the moon and return him safely to earth; his answer was simple and direct: "They will to do it."

President Kennedy never asked if it were possible. He never asked if they could afford it or any one of a thousand other questions, all of which would have, at that time, been valid questions. President Kennedy made a decision. He decided we would put a man on the moon and return him safely to earth before the end of the decade. The fact that it had never been done before in all the hundreds of thousands of years of human history was not even a consideration. He decided where he was with what he had. The objective was accomplished in his mind the second he made the decision. It was only a matter of time, which is governed by natural law, before the goal was manifested in form for the whole world to see.

> *In any moment of decision, the best you can do is the right thing, the next best thing is the wrong thing, and the worst thing you can do is nothing.*
> **—President Theodore Roosevelt**

I frequently discuss the law of attraction: everything vibrates, nothing rests—an ocean of motion. That is because we are energy and whatever energy flow we are in (positive or negative) we will attract. Therefore, once you make a definite decision you will attract the people and resources you need. Many people will tell you that's absurd—you can't just decide to do something if you do not have the necessary resources. That is not true.

My favorite part of the power of positive thinking is based upon all the great thinkers and decision makers in history. If you study them you will come to understand that they disagreed on many points when it came to the study of human life; however, there was one point on which they were in complete and unanimous agreement and that was:

We become what we think about.

Let's think about Babe Ruth. Everyone focuses the attention on his achievement of 714 homeruns. However, try to keep in mind that he struck out 1,330 times. Or Thomas Edison finding 10,000 ways a light bulb won't work. He made a sound decision and kept persistent. Once you make a decision, back it with enthusiasm. Getting excited puts you into a positive energy flow.

> *When you're inventing, if you flunk 999 times and succeed once, you're in.*
> **—Charles F. Kettering**

Don't worry about failing. It's just feedback letting you know what modifications you must make in your plan. Once you achieve success you will have learned from your failures. Do not allow others to influence your decisions by discussing why something can't be accomplished. You will just attract more of what you DON'T want. Keep your mind focused on what you DO want. Think about that. When you are attempting to make choices you may find yourself focused on all that could go wrong, and that is focusing on what you do NOT want.

Humanistic psychologist Dr. Abraham Maslow, who devoted his life to studying self-actualized people, stated very clearly that we should follow our inner guide and not be swayed by the opinion of others or outside circumstances. Maslow's research showed that the decision makers in life had a number of things in common. Most importantly, they did work they felt was worthwhile and important. They found work a pleasure, and there was little distinction between work and play. Maslow said that to be self-actualized you must not only do work you consider important, you must do it well and enjoy it. Maslow recorded that these superior performers had values, those qualities in their personalities they considered to be worthwhile and important. Their values were not imposed by society, parents, or other people in their lives. They made their own decisions. Like their work, they chose and developed their values themselves.

Maslow believed that when a human being ascends the hierarchy of needs, one might achieve self-actualization. His interpretation of hierarchy of needs:

- Physiological: breathing, food, water, etc.
- Safety
- Love/belonging
- Esteem
- Self-actualization: morality, creativity, problem solving, lack of prejudice, acceptance of facts

First you must realize that many successful business leaders have made many mistakes on their way up, but they struggle through the failures—the bad decisions—and then move on to eventually find the solution.

What are some common decision-making mistakes?

- Becoming overwhelmed (a major cause of failure). This is where meditation will help. Calmness of mind will provide clarity.

- Relying too much on expert information. Experts are only human like the rest of us. So gather information from multiple sources instead of focusing on just one.

- Overestimating the value. This goes hand-in-hand with the "expert" phenomenon. We place too much value on expert opinion and allow it to sway our decisions. You know your own business—YOU are an EXPERT!

- Perception. If we have expectations that we are not aware of, we tend to see what we want to see. So be aware of your own preconceptions and stay open to everything that comes your way.

- Lack of intuition. Not listening to your gut feelings can be a major mistake. Intuition is your body talking to you. LISTEN to it. Our brains are constantly absorbing more information than we can process; the extra information gets stored in our subconscious. Our body stores it for future use. In the moments when we are required to make a decision our bodies provide clues or "gut feelings." Unfortunately, our society has trained us to ignore these feelings, but following your intuition will prove to better your decision making.

- Missed opportunity. Failing to act on a decision is caused by fear. Remember, fear isn't real (False Evidence Appearing Real). It is something you create in your mind. Even if you fail, it's okay. Failure is good. Welcome it. It is a steppingstone to success.

When making decisions you must take into consideration the skills you have.

What is your skill set? How do you define it? What is the purpose? How does it affect the decision-making process?

These are the most common questions I have encountered; therefore, I will outline a series of steps to help you discover your skill sets. Defining your skill sets will primarily benefit you by discovering your fastest path to cash. Your skill sets differ from your "desires" or "goals." Defining your skill sets is a way for you to discover infinite possibilities to create cash while still devising a plan to make your goal attainable. Note that your current position isn't necessarily indicative of your skill set.

My first suggestion is to make a list of everything about yourself (e.g. hobbies, people skills, what industries you are familiar with), write down what others inquire of you via assistance, then brainstorm with family, friends, and colleagues.

The following is a detailed list which I categorized between personality: common/creative skills; physical/technical; and management/leadership skills.

Personality:

Relationship/Interaction Skills—
interpersonal communication
This establishes productive and positive relationships and increases well-being and satisfaction of others. It helps you develop yourself and allows you to assist others toward personal growth:

- Ability to demonstrate, coach, or train/instruct
  Do you feel as though your personality displays social skills?
  Do you possess the ability to comfortably teach/instruct others in a professional manner?
  Can you exhibit yourself with confident behavior?
- Sensitivity
  Does your sensitivity reveal enough balance to display your emotions while using caution so you do not create additional problems?
- Resolve conflict
  Do you have the ability to provide resolution to opposition and create enough rapport to successfully resolve discrepancies?
- Provide care and support
  Does your character allow you to offer sound advice and reinforce compassion?
- Serve as liaison
  Can you interact between parties without creating misperception?

- Serve clients or customers
  Can you create positive dialog to create customer satisfaction in all areas?

Communication Skills—verbal and written communication
This is the exchange of information through verbal, written, and nonverbal communication. It provides influence and ideas, identifies problems, provides suggestions, and develops solutions:

- Listen, speak, write, or edit
  Which of these communication skills are your strength and clarity? Rate them.
- Persuade, promote, sell, or group speaking
  Using the aforementioned communication skills, how could you effectively target your market?
- Consult, interview, or negotiate
  What communication skills would you utilize to produce effective results?

Common/Creative Skills:

**Analytical Skills—logical processing of data
to produce information for problem solving**
This is the ability to identify and define problems and solutions. It is a compilation and organization of data for planning and effectiveness. It is also being able to perform numerical and statistical calculations to provide useful information.

- Analyze, research, or problem solve
  Are resources readily available for information gathering, and if not, what steps can you take to provide that availability?
- Categorize or evaluate
  Once you've attained the necessary information, are you able to categorize and evaluate relative to importance?
- Data management
  Are you competent enough in your organizational skills to provide data with a managerial approach?
- Budgeting/computing/estimating or forecasting
  Do you have the required aptitude to perform numerical compilations?

Creative Skills—the process and generation of ideas and information

This is the ability to develop and act upon perceptions gained. It is a formation of structures, patterns, and connections from information, images, and ideas. It is having the ability to express a vision into a creative or artistic form.

The following are all vital in the process and generation of ideas and information, so rate them on a scale of importance and strength so you may determine what areas.

- Brainstorm
- Demonstrate foresight
- Use intuition
- Visualize
- Design

- Integrate
- Invent
- Create images
- Perform

Physical/Technical Skills—interaction of the body with physical objects including machinery and technological systems
This is being skillful in using hands and body with precision in a physical setting and being proficient in product assembly. It is returning something to its original state and being skillful in the proper use of tools, hardware, software, equipment.

- Body coordination, hand dexterity
  Research jobs or entrepreneurships where you could use body coordination, and determine if it is an avenue you wish to pursue. There are multiple businesses where this is applicable.
- Outdoor skills
  Environmental opportunities are actually in demand. If this is an area where you could use your skills and find self-satisfaction, then it is worth checking on.
- Building/construction skills
  Inspect, test, install, repair, or operate machinery: make a list of all mechanical, electrical, and construction abilities, and attempt to establish a connection with other skills and experience.
- Artistic—sketch/draw

This proves to be someone who possesses creative skills. Don't just focus on your abilities but also areas of enjoyment. Let's assume you have multiple skill sets and your creativeness will not permit the type of job you need to create a fast path to cash. Well, you can find a position to serve that purpose and use your creative skills to perform an additional source of income as an alternative.

Managerial/Leadership Skills—utilize organizational, managerial, and leadership skills to accomplish goals
This is being able to initiate and structure procedures toward project completion. It is having the ability to motivate individuals/groups toward higher performance levels and create a strategic plan of action to achieve excellence in job performance.

- Coordinate, implement, organize, manage projects
- Coach and develop a team
- Set and reach goals
- Lead and motivate
- Make decisions
- Take initiative

Using the aforementioned categories, write down your skills by placing a number beside the ones that are applicable, in the order of importance. If you find that you have limited communication skills then you should not apply for a position in which you would be responsible for giving presentations. This process will also highlight areas where you require assistance.

Your life is short and important, and you have the potential to do anything you choose. You must make a decision where you are with what you've got. Follow the history of the great leaders in the world and you will realize the importance of making a decision.

Did your decision solve the problem?

Did it move your business forward?

Once you have made a sound decision you must implement the goal-setting process. Goals tie into the process to assist you with continual effort toward making decisions.

Chapter 5
Goals: Eliminate Your Saboteurs

All who have accomplished great things have had a great aim, have fixed their gaze on a goal which was high, one which sometimes seemed impossible.
—Orison Swett Marden

The greater danger for most of us isn't that our aim is too high and we miss it, but that it is too low and we reach it.
—Michelangelo

N ow that you've made a sound decision, you must put into place a strategic plan of action to set and reach your goal. So what is a goal? It is a dream, a vision of where you want to be, what you want to accomplish.

Many clients come to me for executive coaching, and in the process I sometimes discover that they have no personal goal. A person without goals is lost. Usually a person without a goal has many fears and blocks. I previously discussed how fear could cripple us. It prohibits you from dreaming.

Having a goal offers the following benefits:

- A goal is used as a tool to guide you. Make sure it is something you really desire. Make it a BIG goal. One that scares you.
- A goal will create an awareness of your strengths and weaknesses. Goal planning will allow you to identify your PA (Productive Actions) and NPA (Non-productive Actions).
- A goal will guide your behavior. You can't contradict what you are able to afford; therefore, your goal must be aligned with your budget.
- A goal will provide you with challenges. This is part of your action plan.
- A goal will require you to get organized. Write it out and then pull in your visualization techniques.
- A goal will help to eliminate procrastination, improve performance, and intensify motivation and persistence. These go hand-in-hand. You will need an accountability partner. This will increase your motivation, and you will then make it part of your routine. Motivation is a golden rule in goal setting.

- A goal will increase your self-esteem. Once you have a clear direction it will affect how you see yourself. You will begin to recognize success from within.
- A goal will help you develop a better attitude—an attitude of gratitude.
- A goal will decrease negativity and increase positivity. They go together. Giving yourself positive instructions helps make it a reality.

Positive affirmations are very important. See yourself as if you've already achieved your goal. Also, align your goal with all areas of your life. For example:

- Think about your family and how you will balance your career with family obligations.
- How will it affect your spiritual and financial life? Money tends to be a problematic area for many people. Understanding and implementing faith will help you reach your goal without fear.
- Will it impact you physically? It is imperative to instill good health habits.
- If your educational background is not in alignment with your goal, what resources will you need?
- Does your present career serve you, or do you need to make a change?
- Are you able to grow in your present state?
- Do your relationships impact your mood, career, health, etc.?

Make sure your goal is a SMART goal:

- Specific. Write down all details.
- Measurable. Set a solid dollar figure you desire.
- Attainable. If it is an impossibility to achieve you will shut down.
- Realistic. The goal has to be relevant to your skill sets.
- Timely. Set deadlines so it pushes you forward.

Goals allow you to achieve unlimited success in every aspect of your life. Successful people radiate self-confidence. They expect success and they get success. Why? Because they set and reach goals. Goal achievers reach their true potential because their attitude of gratitude attracts success.

So how long do I give myself? Learn how to set and reach personal and professional goals, and list them as short and long term. One-, five-, ten-, and twenty-year goals are categorized differently and will keep things in perspective. The moment you consciously entertain the image of yourself in possession of your goal you have it on the first level of creation, which is the intellectual level. You plant the seed with visualization and then get emotionally involved in it. The moment you get emotionally involved with your goal, the image automatically begins to move into physical form. Remember that happiness and peace of mind are not goals. They are conditions of life and the result of a higher degree of awareness, which will affect your goals. Two universal laws will affect you in setting and reaching goals:

- Law of cause and effect: every cause has an effect and every effect has a cause. There is no such thing as chance. It's not a miracle, chance, or luck. Ralph Waldo Emerson said this law is the law of laws. Wallace Wattles talks about how like causes produce like effects. As you sow so shall you reap. Concentrate on the cause (material income, health, respect, etc.) and the effect will take care of itself.

- Law of gender: misunderstanding this law causes many people to feel as though they failed. All things are manifested as masculine and feminine. This law governs creation. It completes the seven subsidiary laws. Everything is male and female and is required for existence. The second part of this law states that all seeds have an incubation period before they manifest. Ideas are spiritual seeds! When you envision a dream or goal in your mind, a definite period of time must elapse before it's manifested in physical form. All ideas move into form on an intellectual level as soon as you think about them. As you turn the idea over to your emotional mind it becomes physically manifested. You don't know how long it will take in the gestation period.

Achieving a goal is a creative process. The first step in the creation of your goal takes place in your subconscious mind. Through the aid of your senses and your imagination, you must form a very clear, concise image of yourself already in possession of your goal. This image or picture should then be written with words in as much detail as possible. Making a clear, concise written description of your goal will help clarify and crystallize the image in your subconscious mind.

Picture or imagine your goal in the present tense, as if you have already achieved it. You actually have your goal on a conscious level; therefore, you must begin thinking and talking as though you've already attained your goal. Consciously reaffirming your goal by rewriting your image as often as possible will strengthen the image in your mind. Remember, your conscious mind is your reasoning mind, which means you have the ability to accept or reject any thought at the conscious level. However, once you have accepted it then it goes into the subconscious mind (which does not reason). It doesn't care if it is a positive or negative thought. It then produces your actions. So be careful what you accept.

Bob Proctor shared the following with me, and I would like to pass it on to you. Written by Genevieve Behrend, it is titled "Your Invisible Power."

Order Of Visualization:

The exercise of the visualizing faculty keeps your mind in order, and attracts to you the things you need to make life more enjoyable, in an orderly way. If you train yourself in the practice of deliberately picturing your desire and carefully examining your picture, you will soon find that your thoughts and desires proceed in a more orderly procession than ever before.

Having reached a state of ordered mentality, you are no longer in a constant state of mental hurry. 'Hurry' is 'Fear,' and consequently destructive. In other words, when your understanding grasps the power to visualize your heart's desire and holds it with your will, it attracts to you all things requisite to the fulfillment of that picture, by the harmonious vibrations of the law of attraction. You realize that since Order is Heaven's first law, and visualization places things in their natural order, then it must be a heavenly thing to visualize. Everyone visualizes, whether they know it or not. Visualizing is the great secret of success.

The conscious use of this great power attracts to you multiplied resources, intensifies your wisdom, and enables you to make use of advantages which you formerly failed to recognize.

Visualization and the discovery between creative and real:

We all see the world from our own individual perceptions—meaning you hear what you want to hear and believe what you choose to believe. You possess a force within you to make the choices of that which you desire. Did you ever wonder if the surroundings in our waking consciousness could be a creation in our minds, just as in our dreams? Many scientists believe you will find the good things you desire if you put them into your surroundings and can eliminate the evil ones you fear. Thoughts are creative, thus giving you the ability to create that which you desire. Psychology educates us to comprehend that each one of us has the power within to become what he desires.

When you recognize and comprehend the universal truth that your mind has the same properties as the universal mind, you will see your life transform in miraculous ways. It is not a philosophical ideal passed down, but an exact scientific truth—know it, believe it, and apply it. The universal mind goes by many names (e.g. scientifically, unified field; spiritually, God, etc.). However, the name is relevant only insofar as it resonates with you.

The nature of the universe is:

- Omniscient (all knowing—having infinite knowledge)
- Omnipotent (all powerful—having unlimited power)
- Omnificent (all creative—unlimited powers of creation)
- Omnipresent (always present—in all places at the same time)

The same is true for your own mind; you have access to all knowledge, infinite power, limitless creativity, and it's present in all places at the same time. There is profound truth in the ancient teaching that we are all one, all connected—not only to each other but to all of nature and to everything in the universe.

For a moment, reflect on the modern comforts of our lives: airplanes, trains, electricity, automobiles, etc. They were created by 2 percent of our population. Were they rich, educated, sons of wealth? No; most of them had no or minimal formal education, and some were even labeled as ignorant. They accomplished by the genius creation of their minds. Think about it: Walt Disney was fired by a newspaper editor because "he lacked imagination and had no good ideas." He went bankrupt several times before he built Disneyland. In fact, the proposed park was rejected by the city of Anaheim on the grounds that it would only attract riffraff. Yet who has more creative imagination than Walt Disney?

> *The possibilities of creative effort connected with the subconscious mind are stupendous and imponderable. They inspire one with awe.*
>
> **—Napoleon Hill**

Creative imagination, autosuggestion, and all self-administered stimuli that reach one's mind through the five senses is the agency of communication between that part of the mind where conscious thought takes place and that which serves as the seat of action for the subconscious mind. No thought can enter the subconscious mind without the aid of the principle of autosuggestion. In relaxation therapy and neurolinguistic programming (NLP) we teach tools and techniques that use this method. It is a proven therapeutic tool for overcoming negativity. Creative imagination is the "receiving set of the brain." Using your senses with creative imagination helps a thought or goal to become a reality.

You are like a radio receiving station in that you can tune in to whatever you like—happiness or sadness, success or failure, optimism or fear. With relaxation therapy, the client is given suggestions upon reaching the theta state, which is the part of the session that delivers the therapeutic message. This technique helps to promote accelerated human change. Suggestion creates desired changes in behavior and encourages mental and physical well-being.

There are multiple relaxation techniques:

- Relaxation therapy
- Massage therapy

- Tai Chi
- Yoga
- Zero gravity

Some techniques require you to use both visual imagery and body awareness. For instance, when you are striving to reduce stress, you would use an autogenic relaxation technique in which you repeat words or suggestions in your mind to relax and reduce muscle tension. Nature has built man so that he has absolute control over the information that reaches his subconscious mind through his five senses. Then there are visualization techniques in which you form mental images to take a visual journey to a peaceful, calming place or situation. If you use a progressive muscle relaxation exercise you would focus on slowly tensing and then relaxing each muscle group.

Remember, the more detailed your image of your goal, the faster your subconscious mind will create and deliver the changes you desire.

There are multiple benefits of visualization that include improvements in our health. When we learn the techniques it aids in the visualization process, but it also promotes a healthier lifestyle.

Some of the benefits include:

- Slowing down your heart rate
- Lowering your blood pressure
- Slowing down your breathing rate
- Increasing blood flow to major muscles

- Reducing muscle tension and chronic pain
- Improving concentration
- Reducing anger and frustration
- Boosting confidence for effective problem solving

Visualization is one of the greatest secrets of success. It must be applied in an orderly manner so you can eliminate confusion. Confusion places you in a state of mental acceleration, which ultimately causes fear.

The very first step in a relaxation process is controlled breathing. Whether you are in a severe state of panic or experiencing slight anxiety, you can learn how to breathe to relieve that anxiousness. Take ten minutes and perform the following breathing and relaxation technique:

- Close your eyes
- Take a deep breath in through your nose, very deep
- Hold it as long as you are able
- Exhale *very* slowly
- Repeat this three times
- Again—same process
- Feel yourself relaxing, from the top of your head to the tips of your toes
- Go through the feeling for each body part, talk to yourself, then become totally relaxed. The part of the breathing technique that provides calmness is when you exhale. However, that's why it is important to breathe in through your nose very deeply. You need enough air to expel.

Breathing is very beneficial, and the most important aspect is to let it out as slowly as you can. This is the calming part, and that is why you need to take a very deep breath in. The deeper you breathe the more you have to expel.

Now, incorporate this into the visionary part of your goal and utilize your senses:

- Recite the words you wrote on your card
- With your eyes closed, envision what it is that you desire—do not leave out any details
- When picturing every detail, look around at what you envision
- What smells are lingering?
- What sounds resonate in your mind?
- What is appearing in your vision that you can taste?
- What objects can you touch in the picture?
- What do they feel like?
- Now . . .
- Make it REAL

Learning how to utilize your senses takes practice. While you are sitting down to rent a movie, watch it a second and third time. Pay attention to the details: What background noises do you hear? What items are displayed in the background? Be attentive to what is going on around the actual movie. This will allow you to become in-tune with your senses. Try it on several occasions (e.g. when you go to dinner observe behavioral patterns of others, look and listen to your surroundings; maybe it's on a bus or in a store). Start to be attentive to your surroundings and it will help you in your imaginative duties. See yourself rendering the service you intend to give.

> *Formulate and stamp indelibly on your mind a mental picture of yourself as succeeding. Hold this picture tenaciously and never permit it to fade. Your mind will seek to develop this picture!*
> **—Dr. Norman Vincent Peale**

It is imperative to remember the importance of your thoughts.

> *If you think you are beaten, you are;*
> *If you think you dare not, you don't.*
> *If you'd like to win, but think you can't*
> *It's almost a cinch you won't.*
> *If you think you'll lose, you've lost.*
> *For out in the world we find*
> *Success begins with a fellow's will:*
> *It's all in his state of mind.*
> *If you think you're outclassed, you are:*
> *You've got to think high to rise,*
> *You've got to be sure of yourself before*
> *You'll ever win that prize.*
> *Life's battles don't always go*
> *To the stronger or faster man,*
> *But sooner or later the man who wins*
> *Is the one who thinks he can.*
> —Attributed to author **Napoleon Hill** circa 1973

An additional area of focus, relative to creative imagination, is found in business. In the book *The Science of Getting Rich* Wallace Wattles clearly differentiates the difference between the creative mind and the competitive mind. Dr. Joseph Murphy explains Wattles' message very clearly.

He states:

> There is a thinking stuff from which all things are made, and which, in its original state, permeates, penetrates, and fills the inter-spaces of the universe. A thought in this substance produces the thing that is imaged by the thought. Man can form things in his thought, and by impressing his thought upon formless substance can cause the thing he thinks about to be created. In order to do this, man must pass from the competitive to the creative mind; otherwise he cannot be in harmony with the Formless Intelligence, which is always creative and never competitive in spirit.

It is imperative to understand the difference and how to integrate it with the principles. The creative mind is harmonious with the universe and operates from the perspective of infinite abundance. The essence of Wattles' message is that you will enjoy success by transcending your competitive mind and instead operating from the realm of your creative mind. Being in the creative mindset places you on the path to fulfilling your purpose and living your dream while being of service to others. You become intent on leaving a positive impression, performing to the best of your ability, and providing the best service for others toward growth and expansion. Wattles' teachings enforce the law of reciprocity: you get back what you give.

The majority of us operate from our competitive mind, leading us to a natural sense of distrust and inherent competition in everything we think or do. We mentally perceive that resources are scarce, times are tough, and there must be winners and losers. Operating from the competitive mind creates focus on our own wants and needs—what's in it for me. Competitively focusing on others, fearing the competition, or feeling as though there isn't enough abundance for everyone will surely keep you from operating in the creative mindset.

I've personally had the pleasure of meeting other entrepreneurs of equal commerce who fully comprehend this logic and have put forth the effort to help me in my endeavors. Do not fear competition, and realize that you will be rewarded for helping those who are attempting to "create" their own entrepreneurship. Factually stated, it builds rapport and affiliations within the business community. Opportunities begin to occur that benefit multiple associates. Eliminate the fear of competition and come to the aid of the individual who is where you once were.

Always set short- and long-term goals. Remember to express those goals by maintaining a vision. Your short-term goals will keep you on course.

On the cover of the Revolutionize Your Life series of my books is a flower from Vincent van Gogh's tree. I've always been very impressed with his work. He once said, "I dream my painting and then I paint my dream." He knew his purpose in life. His vision, then, was the completion of paintings, each uniquely different from the other. How he put his vision to canvas involved a series of short-term goals.

Once you've visualized your goal it's time to plot your course and continue with additional goal planning. Achieving your goals means you are a professional. A person who achieves their goals is never in a state of hurry, rush, or panic. These states cause confusion. In contrast a goal achiever always has a lot to do, knows how to get it done, and completes their projects in a calm, confident manner.

Remember, a goal is something you go after that you haven't done before. There are three types of goals:

- Type A: something you already know, your present results
- Type B: something you think you could do
- Type C: something you desire—a fantasy

Bob Proctor taught me that to build your fantasy, you have to move it to a theory and then get emotionally involved in it. The expression of your emotional involvement is going to change your behavior. As your behavior changes, your theory then turns to fact. It works. I have personally achieved success.

Millions of people are held back from success because they do not know how to get things done. They "almost" get things done. The "almosts" are not lazy. They just don't know how to effectively get things done.

***YOU DON'T HAVE TO WORK HARDER—
YOU JUST NEED TO WORK SMARTER!***

Those who are able to reach their goals do a tremendous amount of work in a minimal amount of time. They are not busy for the sake of busy-ness; rather they are effective. They rarely rush and are seldom in a panic. Hurry, rush, and panic are mental states that individuals who do not have a goal experience whenever they have a lot to do. It creates confusion, whereas elimination of these negative states allows the professional to accomplish things productively.

Once you come up with your plan of action for setting and reaching goals, you need to back it with a definiteness of purpose and faith. Reflect on your behavioral patterns—your multitude of habits. That is your paradigm.

So what would a corporate paradigm be, and how does it affect your career?

Chapter 6
A Healthy Corporate Paradigm

To ignore the power of paradigms to influence your judgment is to put yourself at significant risk when exploring the future. To be able to shape your future you have to be ready and able to change your paradigm.
—Joel Barker

Chains of habit are too light to be felt until they are too heavy to be broken.
—Warren Buffet

W hat is a paradigm?
A paradigm is your thinking model, your thought pattern—A MULTITUDE OF HABITS

EXPRESSED IN BEHAVIORAL PATTERNS. When we were born we all started out the same. But over time we developed a paradigm, a way of thinking. Throughout our lives so many things are impressed into our paradigm (the media, our parents, friends, etc.) that it is very difficult to change. What we have come to believe, we believe.

A habit is an idea that is fixed in a person's subconscious mind that causes them to do something without any conscious thought. A paradigm is what causes our habitual behavior. I did not fully comprehend paradigms until I met Bob Proctor, and then after careful study and years of experience I learned how to change those unwanted behaviors and habits. My instructor, Dr. Steve Jones, also helped me to accelerate those changes.

At times we do things we do not want to do, get results we do not want, but we do it anyway. This is because of the paradigm in the subconscious mind that controls our actions or behaviors. For a person to experience permanent change in their personal or professional life, there must be a change in the primary cause of their results. A common error is trying to change results by changing behavior. When this happens, the change is generally temporary. Although behavior causes results, it is a secondary cause. The primary cause is the paradigm. If we understand paradigm, we begin to understand the power of habit. We can change when we understand how the subconscious mind is programmed.

Do you ever wonder why a person of average intelligence can produce extraordinary results? Those individuals have changed their paradigm consciously and subconsciously.

Clearly understand that when you have an awareness of how the paradigm functions, you can start taking control of the results you are getting and go after the goals you desire.

Once you override your old paradigm you will encounter exponential growth. However, you must keep in mind how powerful paradigms are. They have the tendency to talk you out of doing the very things that you decide to do. This is where persistence comes in. Your paradigm returns what it knows. If you experience fear, worry, or doubt relative to finance (i.e. poverty, bankruptcy, etc.) your subconscious mind will surely deliver.

Once you implement the visioneering process, make a decision, and begin goal planning, you are on the mental highway for changing your paradigm. Changing our habits takes time, energy, and focus. It's a reprogramming process. Simply identifying your limiting ability is not enough because that won't change it. You need to fully comprehend how to alter it. You do this by discipline.

So, what is the difference between paradigms and corporate paradigms? Well, a corporate paradigm could also be called corporate culture. It is a group habit or a multitude of habits. In this scenario you must transform the team habits by first identifying them.

Pros/Cons of Workplace Habits:

- Organizational habits impact your career success.
- Procrastination will not permit you to move into a decision-making role.

- Consistency is best. If late assignments or poor work quality become habitual they will produce a negative attitude that will create major roadblocks to success.
- Mistreating colleagues creates a negative environment.

The working class can become a master class. You are where you are because you do what you do. Opportunity cannot be controlled. You, as a working-class individual, have your future in your own hands, so create the environment and the team that you desire. Your self-image is what you project to the outer world and assists you with producing positive results. A confident person understands their self and has a good image of who they are; whereas an insecure person is critical of others and has a poor self-image. Your self-image combined with your behavioral patterns is your paradigm.

So, how do we begin to change our self-image?

Think about who you want to be and what is the desired outcome. Act as if you have already become the person you want to be and then be good to yourself. Love yourself and reward yourself as you make positive changes. Surround yourself with likeminded people who can assist you with positive changes. You also have an outer image, which is how you project yourself to the outer world by the way you look, dress, and act.

An example of a positive corporate paradigm is a team that works together to improve performance. They produce a fast-moving, powerful, and profitable organization once they recognize and change negative behavioral patterns. When you have a team that operates in a spirit of harmony toward the same objective, you have one of the most powerful forces in the world.

A few positive results of forming new habits:

- Establishes effective work habits
- Enhances personal and professional success
- Creates a positive work environment
- Provides accountability. Sometimes you are too close to the situation and don't realize the impact your actions have on the organization.
- Identifies positive implications for forming your new habit
- Provides an understanding of how a new habit benefits you and the organization

It takes a minimum of thirty days for change to take place in the subconscious mind. Many behavioral changes fail. In a corporate environment, this causes significant financial burdens as well as loss of time and productivity. Sometimes it's caused by lack of commitment from senior executives. Multiple changes can result in confusion and commitment.

Your conscious mind is the porter at the door, the watchman at the gate. It is to the conscious mind that the subconscious mind looks for all its impressions.
—Robert Collier

Are your present surroundings discouraging you from your real potential?

Do you feel if you had the ability to change your current situation that success would be easier for you to attain?

Just assume that your real environment is within you and all the factors of success or failure are in your inner world. I've experienced numerous failures within my own life; however, I have reached the realization that you can't fail as long as you are willing to begin again. Rebuild your empire without seeking permission from others. Your belief is your power to attain anything you desire. Remain congruent with your confidence and the universe will return what you are asking for in greater abundance.

So, with that in mind, let's begin by discussing the psychological filtering system. The subconscious mind seeks familiarity at an unconscious level. Your behavior stems from your youth. Understanding the developmental periods of a child's life will help you comprehend where your habits derived from.

- From birth to age 7: this is the imprint level during which sensory information is constantly being imprinted. The child soaks up information from the environment.
- Ages 7 - 14: this is the modeling period where children model and imitate behavioral patterns of others. They unconsciously imitate celebrities, friends, and parents.
- Ages 14 - 21: this is where they unconsciously determine what's important to them. Also known as the socialization period. They break away from the modeling period

As you understand the developmental periods you must also understand how the mind works. The mind affects your every decision. You have a conscious mind and a subconscious mind. Your conscious mind is your reasoning mind. It has the ability to accept or reject any thought on the conscious level. HOWEVER, once you accept a thought to be true it goes into the subconscious mind, and that is what produces your results. Remember, your subconscious mind cannot reason. It accepts whatever is in there to be true. I repeat this statement throughout my book so it will resonate with you. It is very important to understand this.

Whether applicable to chemistry, physics, or mathematics, there are basic principles in life. They do not differ from the principles of your subconscious mind. Research has shown that the ability to bring into action the subconscious power has determined the success of all the great scientists. Sir Isaac Newton's law of universal gravitation states: Every object in the universe attracts every other object with a force directed along the line of centers for the two objects that is proportional to the product of their masses and inversely proportional to the square of the separation between the two objects.

Albert Einstein's theory of relativity and mass-energy equivalence is his most famous equation, $E=mc2$. That equation, written in that form, immediately suggests the possibility of converting small quantities of mass into large quantities of energy. He wanted to explain the existence of mass, of matter. Simply put: our entire existence. Many different forces govern our universe scientifically. Examples of two of these forces are the force of gravity, which holds planets together, and electromagnetic force, which holds tiny particles like atoms together. Einstein's theory of relativity is one of the most astounding scientific breakthroughs of all time.

What is the law of attraction? Everyone's perception of the law of attraction varies. In basic summary, what you put out there is what you'll get back, and when you get it back it will be more powerful—positive or negative. It is a metaphysical "new thought" belief that like attracts like. It is visualization, meditation, spirituality, quantum physics, and energy flow. Scientifically, it would be conceived in the areas of energy and quantum physics. Quantum physics is a branch of science that deals with discrete, indivisible units of energy called quanta as described by the quantum theory. It shows us how we are part of one continuous energy field that we affect with our thoughts—literally creating matter out of light energy. It suggests the probability that universal energy waves have intelligence.

- It is a universal truth that if you drop an object from the top of a building it will fall to the ground.
- It is also a universal truth that matter expands when it is heated. You can heat a piece of steel and it will expand regardless of where it is in the world.
- It is a universal law that action begets reaction—your thought is action and reaction is the automatic response from your subconscious mind, which corresponds with the nature of your thought.

Be careful what you think about!!

The law of attraction or vibration is a conscious awareness that your vibration is in feeling. Once your mind is in movement you will attract whatever vibration you are in. All communication is based on the law of vibration, which can affect you immensely if you are in a sales position. Remember, action and attraction! Everything in the universe vibrates—nothing rests. Use it to pick up another's vibration (intuition). Do not allow negative energy to affect your own vibration. Thoughts are vibrations sent off to the universe, and when you concentrate they get stronger—cosmic waves of energy that penetrate time and space.

Your thought controls the vibration your physical body is in. Your brain is your vibration switching station. Your brain will not think but you think with your brain. Use it to improve your life. When you say you're thinking you are choosing to activate certain brain cells. They in turn affect your central nervous system and you move into whatever vibration those particular cells govern. The law of attraction immediately begins to deliver what you are thinking about. Your mental images are stored in your brain cells. To live in harmony with this law, choose happy pictures! If you're not feeling good, become aware of what you are thinking. Then improve it.

Like the law of attraction, you also have the law of rhythm: everything is moving up and down, to and from, high and low, swinging backward and forward. Remember, there is always a reaction to every action. It is universal: the rising and setting of the sun, the coming and going of the seasons, the flowing in and out of the tides. Similarly, there is a rhythmic swing of consciousness and unconsciousness—your low feelings are what permit you to feel the high feelings. There will always be highs and lows in life. Reason gives us the ability to choose our thoughts (free will!). Everyone experiences low points, but you have the free will to focus on the high points.

In President Nixon's resignation speech, he stated, "It's only by experiencing the depths of the valley that you will enjoy the magnificence of the mountain." To live in harmony with this law think of the good times coming. Even if you are on a down swing, don't feel bad. Know that by law, the swing will change and things can only get better—embrace this law.

> *The subjective mind is entirely under the control of the objective mind. With the utmost fidelity it reproduces and works out to its final consequences whatever the objective mind impresses upon it.*
> —**Thomas Troward**

Your subconscious mind is oftentimes referred to as your subjective mind. It takes cognizance of its environment by means of the five senses:

- Visual (sight)
- Auditory (sound)
- Kinesthetic (touch)
- Gustatory (taste)
- Olfactory (smell)

Your subconscious mind cannot differentiate positive from negative—good from bad. Therefore, it will accept your suggestions without controversy. It is the soil in which you plant the seed. With that being said, you must realize that the main function of your conscious mind should now be to protect your subconscious mind from negativity. Make this your goal, and attempt to turn negative statements and behavior into positives.

Associate that fact with the law of psychological reciprocity: you get back what you give. When you put a positive out you will get a positive back, but rarely right away. However, when you put a negative out you'll get one right back. When someone gives you a positive, give them one right back, and when someone gives you a negative, step aside and let it keep on going. Bob Proctor compares it metaphorically to martial arts. Karate: you hit me—I hit you; you kick me—I kick you. Judo: take the strength of another person's shot and put them down with it. You win the battle but lose the war. Aikido: when someone takes a shot at you, you duck and let it keep on going. This repeats until they've worn themselves out. You're fresh and you can lead them to where you want them to go. When you compliment they'll send good vibrations back, but when you yell at someone and treat them improperly they'll yell back. To live in harmony with this law, never worry about what you are going to get; just concentrate on what you can give. Remember, energy returns to its source of origination.

Why is it that our perception varies so much from person to person? You can place two people at the same seminar, interview both of them afterwards, and their perceptions will be complete opposites. There are numerous documented cases relative to that theory. Two sons grew up with the same alcoholic and abusive father; one grew up to be on drugs, alcohol dependent, and in and out of prison while the other grew up to be a wonderful family man, who never drank alcohol, with a great career. In an interview they both said the reason they became the men they are was due to their father's upbringing. So, do you see? One, blaming the father, grew up to be just like him while the other learned from the father's mistakes to grow up to be the opposite.

Changing your paradigm (your thinking model, your thought pattern, your self-image, your subconscious mind) is a very complicated task. As previously stated, your subconscious mind accepts what has been impressed on it. Earl Nightingale's *The Strangest Secret* talks about the statistics of one hundred men all starting "even" at the age of twenty-five, and by the age of sixty-five only one will be rich. Think about that . . . what happens to most people throughout their lives? Through the course of our lives so many things are impressed into it (e.g. the media, our parents, friends, etc.), so it is very difficult to change it. What we have come to believe, we believe. It returns what it knows. Also, what most educators fail to tell you is that when you discover the required steps to change your subconscious thinking, **you must mean it.** If your actions are not faithful, your subconscious recognizes the false pretense and you'll attract additional negativity. You must learn how to trust in the power, erase negativity, and apply the principles. This is why most people do not believe in the law of attraction and prevent achievement of their goals. The majority of people believe that repetitive conversation in a positive manner produces instant results. However, if the underlying part of your subconscious mind continues to believe your old habits, it is imperative to alter your thought process.

It is very complicated to redirect frustration from your mind, but using the skills in NLP and relaxation therapy produces significant results by accelerating change. The combination of their therapeutic value helps you move toward tranquility. Mastering the tools and techniques for relaxation allows you to apply the necessary steps toward autosuggestion. Calming your body and mind opens the channels toward redirection. I created an internal motivation for the application of the process by realizing the importance of change. It is normal to internally challenge the validity of a positive outcome; however, reinstating the wonderful qualities you will possess will help you in your endeavor to eliminate anger, negative behavioral patterns, undesirable conversation, and unnecessary influence. Trust me, this is factual.

Let's talk about indecision, doubt, and fear, which are the origin of most people's problems. As I previously stated, indecision is the seedling of fear; indecision crystallizes into doubt; and the two blended together become fear—fear being the most crippling. There are six **basic** fears, but many of us do not understand the level of each. These subtle enemies remain hidden in the subconscious mind, where they are difficult to locate, and still more difficult to eliminate. Napoleon Hill discussed them in his book, *"Think and Grow Rich."* Since I've read them I have implemented the teachings to many. Please read over them and write down the ones you have so you will know what obstacles are holding you back. I have students place them on index cards and when they have a negative occurrence I have them place it under the fear that applies to that particular negative.

1. **Fear of Poverty:** When we discuss riches, it doesn't necessarily mean monetary. It means the combination of finance, spirituality, and mental and material estates. This fear paralyzes the faculty of reason, destroys the faculty of imagination, kills off self-reliance, undermines enthusiasm, discourages initiative, leads to uncertainty of purpose, encourages procrastination, and makes self-control an impossibility. This is the most destructive fear.

   Symptoms:
   - Indifference: lack of ambition; willingness to tolerate poverty; acceptance of whatever compensation life may offer without protest; mental and physical laziness; lack of initiative, imagination, enthusiasm, and self-control.
   - Indecision: habit of permitting others to do one's thinking.
   - Doubt: generally expressed through alibis and excuses designed to cover up, explain away, or apologize for one's failures; sometimes expressed in the form of envy of those who are successful, or by criticizing them.
   - Worry: finding fault with others, spending beyond one's income, neglecting personal appearance, scowling and frowning; intemperance in the use of alcoholic drink.
   - Over-caution: looking for the negative side of every circumstance; waiting for the "right time" for putting ideas into action; remembering

those who failed instead of those who have succeeded; pessimism.

- Procrastination: habit of putting off until tomorrow that which should have been done today; alibis and excuses; refusal to accept responsibility; planning what to do in case of failure instead of burning all bridges and making retreat impossible; lack of self-confidence, definiteness of purpose, self-control, initiative, enthusiasm, ambition, thrift, and sound reasoning ability.
- Expecting poverty instead of demanding riches.

2. **Fear of Criticism:** This fear takes on many forms. It robs us of initiative, destroys power of imagination, limits individuality, takes away self-reliance, and does damage in a hundred other ways. Parents often do their children irreparable damage by criticizing them.

    Symptoms:
    - Self-consciousness: nervousness, timidity in conversation, awkward movement of hand and limbs, shifting eyes.
    - Lack of poise: lack of voice control, nervousness in presence of others, poor body posture and memory.
    - Personality: lack in firm decision, agreeing with others without careful examination of their opinions.

- Inferiority complex: using big words to impress others, boasting imaginary achievements.
- Extravagance: spending beyond one's limits.
- Lack of initiative: failure to embrace opportunities, fear to express opinion, lack of confidence in one's own ideas, giving evasive answers to superiors, hesitancy of manner and speech, deceit in words and actions.
- Lack of ambition: mental and physical laziness, lack of self-assertion, slow in decision making, easily influenced by others, habit of criticizing others, suspicious of others without cause, unwillingness to accept blame.

3. **Fear of Ill-Health:** This fear is traced to both physical and social heredity. Fear of ill-health comes from pictures planted in a person's mind of what may happen if death should overcome them.

Symptoms:

- Autosuggestion: habit of self-suggestion by looking for, and expecting to find, symptoms of disease, "enjoying" imaginary illness, talking to others about operations, accidents, and forms of illness. Experimenting with diets, physical exercises, trying home remedies.
- Hypochondria: habit of talking about illness, concentrating the mind upon disease.
- Exercises: interferes with proper physical exercise and results in overweight.

- Susceptibility: worries about hospital bills, saves money for cemetery lots, burial expenses, etc.
- Self-coddling: habit of making a bid for sympathy, feigning illness to cover plain laziness, lack of ambition.

4. **Fear of Loss of Love:**

   Symptoms:

   - Jealousy: habit of being suspicious of friends and loved ones without reasonable evidence of sufficient grounds, accusing wife or husband of infidelity without grounds.
   - Faultfinding: finding fault with friends, relatives, business associates, and loved ones upon the slightest provocation.
   - Gambling: gambling, stealing, cheating, and taking hazardous chances to provide money for loved ones, with the belief that love can be bought. Insomnia, nervousness, lack of persistence, weakness of will, lack of self-control.

5. **Fear of Old Age:** This comes from man having two sound reasons for his apprehension—one growing out of his distrust of his fellowman, who may seize whatever worldly goods he may possess, and the other arising from the terrible pictures of the world beyond, which were planted in his mind through social heredity before he came into full possession of

his mind. Fearing loss of freedom and independence, as old age may bring with it the loss of both physical and economic freedom.

Symptoms:

- The tendency to slow down and develop an inferiority complex at the age of mental maturity, and speaking apologetically of oneself as "being old" merely because of reaching the age of forty or fifty, instead of reversing the rule and expressing gratitude for having reached the age of wisdom and understanding.

- Habit of killing off initiative, imagination, and self-reliance by falsely believing oneself too old to exercise these qualities.

- Dressing with the aim of trying to appear much younger, and affecting mannerisms of youth, thereby inspiring ridicule by friends and strangers.

6. **Fear of Death:** This is the cruelest of the fears. The thought of eternal punishment not only causes man to fear death, it often causes him to lose reason. It destroys interest in life and makes happiness impossible.

Symptoms:

- The habit of thinking about dying instead of making the most of life, due generally to lack of purpose, or lack of a suitable occupation. The greatest remedy—a burning desire for achievement.

There are also seven major negative emotions (to be avoided at all costs).

The emotions of . . .

- Fear
- Jealousy
- Hatred
- Revenge
- Greed
- Superstition
- Anger

Positive and negative emotions cannot occupy the mind at the same time; therefore, one must dominate. It is your responsibility to have the positive emotions be the dominant ones. There are also seven major positive emotions.

The emotions of . . .

- Desire
- Faith
- Love
- Sex
- Enthusiasm
- Romance
- Hope

Fears cause people to be negative. Fear, worry, and doubt are the most crippling, and they are linked to all aspects of failure. They linger in your subconscious mind to create the domino effect, and they are most commonly associated with poverty. Certain fears are associated with multiple scenarios. You will hear it explained as **F**alse **E**vidence **A**ppearing **R**eal. Try to think of fear as something beneficial, something you need. Don't think of fear as your enemy; you actually need it to grow.

> **Each failure is a trial in an experiment**
> **and an opportunity for growth.**

So acknowledge it, identify the source for creating it, and examine it objectively.

Lack and limitation of current results: if you let your present results be your starting point, you're going to get the same results.

How do we break away?

An idea is a thought or collection of thoughts directed toward a purpose. The starting point is thought. If you realize you don't want your present results, begin with new thoughts of what you really want. Do not let the outside world control you.

James Allen said, "Know the truth and the truth will set you free."

Set yourself free from ignorance.

He also said, "Calmness of mind is one of the beautiful jewels of wisdom. *It is the result of long and p*atient effort in self-control. Its presence is an indication of ripened experience and of a more than ordinary knowledge of the laws and operations of thought. You become calm in the measure that you understand yourself as a thought evolved being. *For such* *knowledge necessitates the understanding of o*thers as the result of thought. And, as you develop a right understanding and see more and more clearly the internal relations of things by the actions of cause and effect you cease to fuss and fume and worry and grieve and remain poised steadfast and serene."

Remember, you have choices. Your future is in your own hands. Take responsibility for your life. Responsibility opens the door and permits you to walk in freedom. When you refuse to accept responsibility for your life you are no longer in control of your future. When you accept responsibility for your life you develop confidence. This takes great courage.

George Bernard Shaw said, "People are always blaming their circumstances for what they are. *I d*on't believe in circumstances. The people who get on in this world are the people who get up and look for the circumstances they want, and, if they can't find them, they make them."

There is a vast difference between being responsible "for" and being responsible "to." Ignorance of this principle will most certainly cause a person to experience the destructive emotions of anger, guilt, and resentment. You are responsible for your own feelings and your own results—not another person's. You may be responsible to another person for one thing or another, but not for another person. The only exception, of course, is when you choose to take on the responsibility of raising children until they reach the age of maturity. In that case, you are both responsible to and for them, until such time as they become responsible for themselves.

Do not have another person take on your responsibilities. It makes you dependent on them. They become the giver and you become the receiver. Your well-being is dependent upon their generosity. Hopefully, at some point, it will become very clear that this kind of behavior only leads to a life of lack, limitation, resentment, and confusion on the parts of both giver and receiver.

Nothing positive comes from the misuse of responsibility. When you take on the responsibility for another person's feelings, results, or actions, you destroy their self-reliance and self-respect.

YOU are responsible for:

- Your happiness
- Your health
- Your wealth
- Your emotional state
- All the results in your life!

Winston Churchill said, "Responsibility is the price of greatness."

All the great men and women of success refused to give up. They believed in who they are and what their true potential is. Their discoveries and inventions resulted from their internal belief that there is no limit to possibilities. Edison refused to admit defeat ten thousand times but persevered in his discovery and revealed that he discovered ten thousand ways a light bulb won't work. The only failure of mind comes from worry, doubt, fear, discord, and desertion.

Once you fully comprehend your paradigm and self-image, you are on the road to exponential growth. To produce that growth you must eliminate fear and back your goals with faith. Once we come face-to-face with success we sometimes become afraid of that success. How do we move forward and eliminate that fear?

Burn those boats and conquer your fears.

Chapter 7
Burn The Boats—
Conquer Your Fears

You will either step forward into GROWTH, or you will step back into SAFETY.
—Abraham Maslow

What would life be if we had no courage to attempt anything?
—Vincent van Gogh

W hat does burning the boats and conquering your fears have in common?

Bob Proctor discusses "the terror barrier" and why it is important to learn how to bust through it. The terror barrier is fear, and most people are afraid of failing. I correlate it to the "Burn the Boats" story:

In the introduction I discussed how the ancient Greek warriors were both feared and respected by their enemies for their reputation of unsurpassed bravery and commitment to victory. Once the warriors arrived on the enemy's shore, the commanders ordered them to "burn the boats." With no boats to retreat to, the army had to be successful to survive. As the soldiers watched the boats burn, they realized there was no turning back—no surrendering. The same stands true in your own life and where you have arrived. That is why I love this story; you have no excuses for failure. You MUST "win" or perish. I have personally used this process to attain victory in my own life. It is a huge leap of faith! Think of all the missed opportunities within your own life because you didn't burn the boats.

Remove those obstacles and excuses;
Storm the shore with a successful attitude;
Let your fear and regret burn with the boat;
Leave it at the bottom of the water.

You will be victorious! Imagine the psychological impact on the soldiers when they realized there was no turning back. It removed any notion of retreat from their hearts and thoughts of surrender from their minds. In your own scenario, you will not battle on the shore, but you will battle in your mind. Also, remember that temporary defeat states that "every failure brings with it the seed of equivalent success."

Temporary defeat is something all successful men have endured. Henry Ford was a poor uneducated man who dreamed of a horseless carriage; Walt Disney was fired for "no imagination" and experienced bankruptcy. When they encountered temporary defeat, it was their burning desire to succeed that led to their successful outcome.

All who succeed in life get off to a bad start and pass through many heartbreaking struggles before they arrive. You may have only small desires, but you must fully comprehend that you need one **intense** desire to accomplish your goals. Concentrate on one definite object—one idea at a time. It is imperative that you understand it's all about concentration. You must become fully absorbed so that you are unaware of your surroundings. Do not confuse desire with imagination.

> Imagination is the dream . . . the vision,
> but desire is the internal will,
> the ongoing OBSESSION,
> so concentrate, focus, feel it
> and **believe** it.

They all work simultaneously. Once you understand the burning desire, you will be excited to realize that you can produce anything you want, be anything you want, and accomplish anything you set out to do, if you hold that desire steady with definiteness of purpose. Conscious desire seldom delivers, but the desire that is impressed upon the subconscious will surely deliver. Once you impress upon it you have opened the door of opportunity, and the door of opportunity is NEVER closed. Remember, there are no limits—no law of limitation—unless you impress upon them.

Aim high! Whatever price you set upon yourself, life will give. Aim for the moon, but if you miss, you will surely hit a star. You are an intelligent, reasoning creature whose mind is part of the universal mind. This is your opportunity for growth, for opportunity.

Berton Braley expressed it well in his poem:

"Opportunity"
For the best verse hasn't been rhymed yet,
The best house hasn't been planned,
The highest peak hasn't been climbed yet,
The mightiest rivers aren't spanned;
Don't worry and fret, faint hearted,
The chances have just begun,
For the best jobs haven't been started,
The work hasn't been done.

I've discussed the importance of understanding the power of the mind throughout all the chapters of this book, and that is because your mind plays a significant role in every aspect of reaching success and happiness. In this chapter I discuss being able to break through to the other side by eliminating fear. This is where we strengthen those mental muscles. What are they?

- Memory: our memory is not imperfect, only weak or strong. We need to learn how to exercise it for strength. Understanding the complexities of the conscious mind and subconscious mind will help with strengthening your memory.

- Reason: our inductive reasoning faculty gives us the ability to originate individual thoughts and bring them together in the formation of ideas.

- Perception: our point of view. Once you are able to change your perception you will be able to change your point of view.

- Imagination: is the most powerful faculty. Everything is built through our imagination. This is why understanding the visualization process is so important to strengthening your imagination muscle. Then it becomes even stronger when you utilize your senses.

- Will-Power: is the ability to hold one picture in your mind for a period of time, which allows you to focus. The more you practice your will the better you will become.

- Intuition: is your sixth sense in which you pick up vibrations and translate them in your mind. It permits you to understand what is going on around you. It is one of your higher faculties and can be developed to an extraordinary degree.

Anytime you set a goal that results in you skipping a couple of rungs on the ladder of success, you will experience the terror barrier. This fear comes from making a serious change in your life by moving out of your comfort zone. We tend to step back into our comfort zone rather than trust and move forward.

With any major change in your behavior, that fear will instantly stand between you and all the good you desire.

Desire

Once you set that vision and make a plan toward your goal, it creates an internal excitement. Then the opportunities will present themselves. Once you acquire that deep-down "burning desire," the opportunities will begin to flourish. Wishing will not bring riches, but desiring riches with a state of mind that becomes an obsession, then planting definite ways and means to acquire riches—and backing those plans with persistence (which does not recognize failure) —will surely produce. Every great leader was a dreamer who had a definiteness of purpose filled with a burning desire to succeed. A burning desire to succeed makes you fully committed, and that is why most people fail to achieve their goals.

Napoleon Hill speaks of the burning desire that Edwin Barnes had inside to become an associate with Edison. He repeatedly recited, "Before I am through I WILL be his associate." It began with a vision he had of himself standing in Edison's presence. He could hear himself asking Edison for an opportunity to carry out the one consuming obsession of his life, a burning desire to become the business associate of the great inventor. When he first envisioned it in his mind, it may have been a wish, but it was no mere wish when he appeared before Edison. It was not hope, but a desire—it was definite. It took five years for something to transpire when he first began to work for Edison, but he succeeded because it was a definite goal backed with all his energy, willpower, and effort. In his own mind Barnes was Edison's partner every minute of the time.

This bears repeating: "wishing" will not bring riches, but "desiring" riches with a state of mind that becomes an obsession, then planning definite ways and means to acquire riches—and backing those plans with persistence (which does not recognize "failure")—will bring riches. Every great leader was a dreamer who had a definiteness of purpose with a burning desire. Copernicus said, "Success requires no apologies, failure permits no alibis."

A burning desire to succeed makes you fully committed, and that is why most people fail to achieve their goals. The most creative dreamers have the determination and commitment to understand that internal belief is unquestionably the power to attain success.

- Abraham Lincoln dreamed of freedom for the black slaves, put his dream into action, and barely missed living to see a united North and South translate his dream into reality.
- The Wright Brothers dreamed of a machine that would fly through the air.

The greatest achievement was, at first and for a time, but a dream.

—Napoleon Hill

To eliminate fear, you must identify and avoid what will sabotage your success. You take your present results and make the decision to make positive improvements, thereby creating new and scary goals. It is easy to create a goal that you know you can accomplish. To meet with the terror barrier means you have set a very big goal that places you outside your comfort level. Comprehension of that permits you to step forward toward growth and freedom. The doubt, fear, and anxiety did not leave; however, through understanding and persistence, you will eliminate them. The discomfort can trigger a limiting and destructive mental process that causes your conscious mind to focus on the negative, which will produce negative results. Those negative thoughts flash upon the screen of your mind and stop you from gaining the freedom you desire.

If you do not learn how to understand what is taking place, you will not reach your desired outcome. If you suppress your anxiety, it is internalized and creates depression. Depression is anger turned inward and is an extremely negative state. One thing I have learned is that you struggle before you arrive. Usually you are at a moment of crisis before the turning point of success. Relate this theory to the universal law of perpetual transmutation—energy flows to and through us. An ocean of motion. Energy moves into physical form and can't be created or destroyed. Thought energy builds ideas then takes the energy and impresses it into the subconscious mind. It then sets up emotion, which in turn produces action. Non-physical life is always moving into physical form. This is part of the creative process. To live in harmony with this law, always be aware (and sometimes BEWARE!) of your thoughts and feelings. If they are anything but pleasing, do whatever you can to make them positive.

The opposite of doubt and worry is understanding that these emotions exist on a conscious level. That understanding leads to an emotional state called faith. Faith is expressed on a physical level as well-being, and that is a good vibration. That good vibration is a motivational force that allows the creative process to accelerate.

Integration of belief with behaviors is part of your paradigm and allows you to be in alignment with your goals. Our belief system is based upon our evaluation of situations, and if we reevaluate those situations then our belief about them will change. Our two levels of belief are processed through our conscious mind, which is logical, and our subconscious mind, which controls our behavior. That behavior is part of the paradigm. At the conscious level we may "think we can"; however, our thoughts at the subconscious level produce our true actions. The thoughts we internalize produce the vibration which causes the action, and—again—that action causes the reaction. Particularly, the law of rhythm.

Once you are able to trust and have faith, you will have exponential growth. You will move to greater heights. You will make a revolutionary change.

Chapter 8
Revolutionary Change

When you come to the edge of all the light you have, and are about to step off into the darkness of the unknown, faith is knowing one of two things will happen: There will be something solid to stand on, or you will be taught how to fly.

—Patrick Overton

After the fact, quantum leaps may be viewed as practical, sensible, even obvious moves, but they typically do not come to you as the obvious moves at the moment. Usually it's in retrospect that you perceive their hidden logic and elegance. Invariably, quantum leaps are not complex or intricate maneuvers. They tend to be simple, energy efficient and time saving.

—Price Pritchett

O ne of the best books I have ever read is called *You2* by Price Pritchett. It is very short but contains powerful information. In it he talks about taking a quantum leap.

So, exactly what is a quantum leap?

Quantum is a word taken from the term "quantum physics." It is an exponential improvement in your performance. It is making a drastic change that is caused from the power of your mind. Most of us go through life making incremental gains in a safe manner; however, a quantum leap takes you from your present level of achievement to higher stages—more quickly.

Many would call this outrageous and say that it contradicts common sense. I think it is brilliant. In *You2* Pritchett discusses different strategies to move you to that higher level. He talks about how "more of the same" just gives you more of the same. How true. Quit trying harder and work smarter. I would like to share a story he writes in the beginning.

I'm sitting in a quiet room at the Millcroft Inn, a peaceful little place hidden back among the pine trees about an hour out of Toronto. It's just past noon, late July, and I'm listening to the desperate sounds of a life-or-death struggle going on a few feet away.

There's a small fly burning out the last of its short life's energies in a futile attempt to fly through the glass of the windowpane. The whining wings tell the poignant story of the fly's strategy—try harder.

But it's not working.

The frenzied effort offers no hope for survival. Ironically, the struggle is part of the trap. It is impossible for the fly to try hard enough to succeed at breaking through the glass. Nevertheless, this little insect has staked its life on reaching its goal through raw effort and determination.

Across the room, ten steps away, the door is open. Ten seconds of flying time and this small creature could reach the outside world it seeks. With only a fraction of the effort now being wasted, it could be free of this self-imposed trap. The breakthrough possibility is there. It would be so easy.

Why doesn't the fly try another approach, something dramatically different? How did it get so locked in on the idea that this particular route, and determined effort, offer the most promise for success? What logic is there in continuing, until death, to seek a breakthrough with "more of the same"?

No doubt this approach makes sense to the fly. Regrettably, it's an idea that will kill.

"Trying harder" isn't necessarily the solution to achieving more. It may not offer any real promise for getting what you want out of life. Sometimes, in fact, it's a big part of the problem.

> If you stake your hopes for a breakthrough on trying harder than ever, you may kill your chances for success.
>
> —**Price Pritchett**, author of *You2*

I love that story and encourage you to purchase his book. It resonates with me because I am someone who continually looks for ideas to work smarter and am not afraid to take risks. I do not take careless risks, but if you wait for 100 percent proof that an exponential move will work in your favor, then you stay stuck in "more of the same." Applying all the principles in the previous chapters will get you to this point. You will be able to take that leap without fear, worry, and doubt.

Taking a quantum leap gives you permission to dream. Set yourself free. He talks about getting rid of your old beliefs. Think back to childhood and your "limiting beliefs." In coaching I teach people to recognize those limiting beliefs and then identify where they came from. Once you figure that out I assist with a plan to release them and then replace the ones that are working against you. If you don't they may sabotage your plan of action and you will encounter new obstacles and challenges. Fear, worry, and doubt hold us hostage. As I previously mentioned, people frequently discuss the "what if's," and that brings doubt. Use it for good. If you are going to doubt something, doubt your limits.

In his book Pritchett talks about something that I teach every day: you don't have to know how you're going to get there, but you need to know where you are going. The first thing is to focus on your dream—your vision. Set your goals and begin working on a strategic plan of action. For the time being stop worrying how you will get there. As we work through a plan you will discover the resources you need to make it happen. Worrying about the "how" will only block you from reaching your desired outcome.

Remember how I discuss following your intuition, your sixth sense? It is an instinctive discovery process based on a sense of direction. Once people work toward a plan of action they are afraid of chaos. We become much more successful when our plan doesn't go according to plan. Encountering obstacles and confusion help us grow. I continually mention that failure is good. It is a steppingstone to success, so once again, welcome it. That is part of opening yourself up to the potential of exponential gains.

We are all afraid to go out of our comfort zone because staying in it ensures we won't have to deal with challenges. If you start to feel uncomfortable, that is a good sign. I believe we all have talents and abilities within us. Once you experience setbacks/failures you will discover talents you didn't realize you had. These new talents and abilities will serve you well. Become passionate about it. Passion fuels the fire. Get emotionally involved in it. That is what places you in a positive energy flow so that you will attract what you need to reach your desired outcome.

One thing Pritchett makes clear in his book is that a quantum leap is not some absurd, wild-eyed scheme that calls for a fantastic stroke of luck just to have an outside chance of working. It is a move that is yours for the taking—a giant step you can make merely by deciding to and opening yourself up to the resources currently available to you. He states, "'Getting ready' is, quite frankly, a stalling tactic, an act of anxiety, a con game you're working on yourself. You are already positioned to escape to a higher plane of performance. If you wait until you can get it perfect, you will never get it at all."

Taking a quantum leap takes faith and intuition. Do you fully comprehend the meaning of faith and the power it produces? It is an earnest desire that we present to God—to the universal mind, to a superior power. Whatever you believe in, as long as it is a higher power, a power for good. It is the desire of our heart and soul. Thoughts, mixed with emotion and faith, immediately translate themselves into their physical equivalent or counterpart. When you are preparing for prayer, ensure that you are alone and have retired to a quiet place where you can concentrate on your thoughts and impress upon your innermost desire with no distractions. It is not enough to impress upon this desire if it is not backed with belief. You must believe that God will grant your prayer.

> **Therefore I tell you . . .**
> **whatever you ask for in prayer,**
> **believe that you have received it,**
> **and it will be yours.**
> **—Mark 11:24**

In my research I have found that science demonstrates the possibility to accomplish anything good, but distrusting your abilities to reach your desired goal will create reservation within you, and failure will be the inevitable result. **Once you fully**

understand that this power is the universal mind and not circumstances or environment, you will surely cause your abilities to surface. There are multiple beliefs throughout the world; however, few will deny the intelligence that governs this universe. I've educated myself to the fact that when you are reading the writings of another, it doesn't matter the title. What matters is, whether referenced as God, universal mind, supreme intelligence, or nature, etc., **it is a force for good.** All of our minds are part of this universal mind just as the sun's rays are part of the sun. We must all be harmonious to attract it for power, and it's insufficient unless you practice it repetitively. Repeated affirmations to your subconscious mind is the only known method of voluntary development of faith.

What is faith?

A state of mind that may be induced, or created, by affirmation or repeated instructions to the subconscious mind through the principle of autosuggestion. It is a state of mind which you may develop at will, after you have mastered the principles associated with the law of attraction. I previously spoke about the law of attraction. It is definitely real because I am living proof of how it works. This is not about saying something positive and then it becomes a reality. It involves applying many principles:

- Visualization
- Relaxation
- Desire
- Faith and intuition
- Autosuggestion/positive affirmations

- Specialized knowledge
- Setting and reaching goals—ACTION
- Persistence, motivation
- Energy—get yourself flowing in a positive energy flow—VIBRATION!
- Then read, write, and repeat!

You must emotionalize your thoughts with feeling and mix them with faith for them to become a reality. Faith is the only known antidote to failure. It is a known fact that love is closely akin to the state of mind known as faith. Take Abraham Lincoln for instance. He failed many, many times until he was well past the age of forty. A nobody from nowhere until a great experience came into his life—Anne Rutledge, the only woman he truly loved. Once she came into his life a sleeping genius was aroused within his heart and brain, thereby giving the world one of its really great men.

In the last chapter, I spoke of the famous terror barrier. Well, it is applicable to the power of faith as well. When you encounter it, you must push through, and you can do it with the application of faith. You must believe that the universal powers will prevail. Experiencing fear of the unknown creates doubt and worry, so search your heart and find your faith.

Happy is the man that finds wisdom,
and the man that gets understanding.
For the gaining of it is better than the gaining of silver,
and the profit thereof than fine gold.
She is more precious than rubies,

and none of the things thou can desire
are to be compared unto her.
Length of days is in her right hand,
in her left hand are riches and honor.
Her ways are ways of pleasantness,
and all her paths are peace.
She is a tree of life to them that lay hold upon her,
and happy is everyone that retains her.
—Proverbs

In the discussion about the book *You2*, I mentioned intuition, or the sixth sense.

We all know and comprehend the power of our five senses: sight (visual), sound (auditory), touch (kinesthetic), smell (olfactory), and taste (gustatory), but what about our sixth sense, intuition? Your sixth sense guides you to keep you out of harm's way by providing a warning. Intuition means inner sight, inner consciousness, inner knowledge. It is defined as "immediate mental apprehension without reasoning; immediate insight." It fills the gap and helps you to attain your desired results.

Did you ever meet someone for the first time and mentally form an assessment, only to find (later) that you were correct?

Did you ever encounter confusion as to which direction to go or how to answer a particular question and your intuitiveness ended up being correct?

Intuition is an unconscious form of knowledge that differs from an opinion, and some refer to it as common sense. It promotes good communication, and the following is a list of ways to improve your intuition:

- Relaxation therapy
- Meditation
- Thinking positive
- Gratitude
- Forgiveness
- Believing in your first impressions
- Staying happy

Failure to act on our intuition doesn't always lead to dramatically tragic endings; however, some degree of adversity is always the result. We are usually led by reason, and this effectively denies our value of faith.

For faith is not a product of reason; faith is the foundation of reason (faith transcends reason) . . . reason always falls into place behind faith.
—Divine Heritage

We would normally act on faith all the time, but our fear of criticism from others prevents us from experiencing those everyday "miracles." It is imperative to understand that things don't have to make immediate sense—this is faith. When you have a vested interest in the outcome of your actions, you are not acting out of faith but out of hope. To desperately seek the truthful outcome, you tend to pursue a certain course of action, and you may confuse the idea of faith with the notion of wishful thinking. So please be careful and recognize the difference.

It is psychological law that whatever we desire to accomplish
we must impress upon the subjective or subconscious mind.
—Orison Swett Marden

The sixth sense is a mixture of mental and spiritual: all groups (e.g. psychiatrists, psychologists, physicians, and churches) use the one universal power resident in the subconscious mind. It is psychic—or paranormality, parapsychology, or spirituality. Even though each may claim the healings are due to their own particular theory, the process of all healing is a definite, positive, mental attitude—namely faith. Regardless of which theory is your own belief, you can rest assured that faith brings results.

We all know the famous saying "The doctor dresses the wound, but God heals it." So you see, it's not the psychologist, psychiatrist, family practitioner, or religious leader who heals the patient. The basic foundation is that they remove the mental or physical blocks so that the healing principle may be released, and the person is healed by the one healing power. The modern mental therapeutic procedure is based upon the truth that the infinite intelligence and power of your subconscious mind responds according to faith. I recently read some corresponding literature from multiple sources that portrayed this same message: "Imagine the ending result of your desire and feel its reality; then the infinite intelligence will respond to your request. This contains the meaning of 'Believe you have received and you shall receive.'" This is what the modern mental scientist does when he practices prayer therapy.

If the Holy Spirit can take over the subconscious with our consent and cooperation, then we have almighty Power working at the basis of our lives, then we can do anything we ought to do, go anywhere we ought to go, and be anything we ought to be.
—**E. Stanley Jones**

The subconscious mind is everywhere and is the creative force of the universe—the eternal energy of God spirit. The name that is placed in writing, relative to the principle of "faith," creates much controversy. Therefore, do not place emphasis on how authors, coaches, mentors, educators, and others categorize faith. You must eliminate the argumentative factors so that you can concentrate on empowering your inner belief. There are multiple types of religion, so to categorize it to one specific religion would cause controversy. For instance, I am of Catholic religion and therefore refer to the faithful power as God, but when teaching the power of faith and the application of this principle, I reference the universe. As I have previously mentioned (multiple times), it only matters to your belief (e.g. universe, supreme intelligence, God, nature, etc.). Keep that in mind and you will eliminate the controversial issues of religion.

It is better to believe than to disbelieve; in so doing, you bring everything to the realm of possibility.
—**Albert Einstein**

Share your faith with others—a harmonious group of likeminded individuals—and create wondrous possibilities. Then back it all with an attitude of gratitude.

Your vibrations—good or bad—will produce exactly that. People take so many things for granted and often fail to be grateful for the "smaller" delights in life. It's similar to resistance vs. persistence. For example: two separate individuals, same circumstance—both have a day at the beach planned, but upon waking in the morning and opening the blinds, they find clouds, wind, and rain. The first individual lets it ruin his day—he is angry, complaining, and sitting around all day long, doing nothing but pouting. The second individual feels some disappointment but immediately turns it around and contemplates gratitude. He realizes they are in desperate need of water, he doesn't have to mow the grass, and he has numerous projects to complete around the house that he has been putting off. So, do you see how you can turn it around?

It is extremely enlightening to comprehend how others have taken detrimental situations and prohibited defeat. I have learned that same principle. Just remember, **every adversity you meet carries with it a seed of equivalent or greater benefit.** Every problem has a solution—you just have to find it! If you develop that "I don't believe in defeat" attitude, you will learn that there is no such thing as defeat, until you accept it as such.

Gratitude needs to be enforced in every aspect of our lives. Your gratitude must come from deep within. I certainly hope that you are already making grateful statements relative to family members, but go beyond that. Wake up being grateful for the day, for the small things, and even for misfortunes. It's much easier to complain, but when you're sincerely applying gratitude, observe how wonderful your day becomes.

Remember, in the application of these principles, trying harder is not necessarily the solution for greater achievement. It is apparent that great advances come about when people have a deep understanding of their true potential and a tremendous desire to lead others to greater levels. We have been programmed to take logical and progressive steps; however, Pritchett's concepts make perfect sense to propel you to exponential gains.

In order to take the quantum leap you will need the assistance of likeminded individuals—a networking group that can provide the necessary resources you will need. In short, you will need to put together the most magnificent team—the mastermind team!

Chapter 9

Mastermind For Success

If you do not believe in cooperation, look what happens to a wagon that loses a wheel.
—Napoleon Hill

Your big opportunity may be right where you are now.
—Napoleon Hill

W hat is masterminding?
This is my favorite subject because it is a powerful tool that can excel you to happiness and success. I have had many mastermind teams throughout my life, and the benefits are great. The concept of the mastermind group was

formally introduced by Napoleon Hill in the early 1900s. In his timeless classic *Think and Grow Rich* he wrote about the Master Mind principle as:

> The coordination of knowledge and effort, in a spirit of harmony, between two or more people, for the attainment of a definite purpose . . . .
>
> No two minds ever come together without thereby creating a third, invisible intangible force, which may be likened to a third mind . . . .
>
> Energy is Nature's universal set of building blocks, out of which she constructs every material thing in the universe, including man, and every form of animal and vegetable life. Through a process, which only Nature completely understands, she translates energy into matter.
>
> Nature's building blocks are available to man, in the energy involved in thinking! Man's brain may be compared to an electric battery. It absorbs energy from the ether, which permeates every atom of matter, and fills the entire universe.
>
> It is a well-known fact that a group of electric batteries will provide more energy than a single battery. It is also a well-known fact that an individual battery will provide energy in proportion to the number and capacity of the cells it contains.
>
> The brain functions in a similar fashion. This accounts for the fact that some brains are more efficient than others, and leads to this significant statement—a

group of brains coordinated (or connected) in a spirit of harmony, will provide more thought-energy than a single brain, just as a group of electric batteries will provide more energy than a single battery.

Through this metaphor it becomes immediately obvious that the Master Mind principle holds the secret of the power wielded by men who surround themselves with other men of brains.

There follows, now, another statement which will lead still nearer to an understanding of the psychic phase of the Master Mind principle: When a group of individual brains are coordinated and function in harmony, the increased energy created through that alliance becomes available to every individual in the group.

Henry Ford began his business career under the handicap of poverty, illiteracy, and ignorance. In the short period of ten years he made himself one of the richest men in America. He formed acquaintances with Edison, Firestone, Burroughs, and Burbank, which provides additional evidence of the power that is produced through harmonious minds.

Economic advantages may be created by any person who surrounds himself with the advice, counsel, and personal cooperation of a perfect harmony. This form of cooperative alliance has been the basis of nearly every great fortune.

Andrew Carnegie surrounded himself with a group of fifty men for the definite purpose of manufacturing and marketing steel. He attributed his entire fortune to the power he accumulated through this mastermind group.

Mastermind groups create a win-win situation for all who participate by developing new friendships and business opportunities. The interaction of the participants creates energy and provides commitment and excitement.

A mastermind group:

- Challenges each other to create and implement goals, then holds you accountable.
- Allows you to brainstorm ideas and provides support backed with total honesty, respect, and compassion.
- Promotes growth and expansion in your business and personal life.
- Creates increased energy.
- Enhances interpersonal relations.
- Fosters an extension of your intelligence.
- Provides a reference point of expectations.
- Allows participants to support each other.

This alliance between the minds is like having your own objective board of directors.

The agenda belongs to the group, and each person's participation is key because collectively you rely on their feedback, brainstorm new possibilities, and set up accountability structures that keep you focused and on track. The possibilities are endless and will move you to greater heights for growth and improvement in your business and personal life. I have been involved with three different mastermind groups throughout my life, and the results were amazing. Imagine placing Einstein, Ford, Edison, and the Wright Brothers in a mastermind group? The organized and intelligently directed knowledge could lead to infinite possibilities.

The groups I have been involved in were from all over the world. I was fortunate enough to have a coach or mentor choose the groups through their organization, so the screening process was already complete. If you are looking to form your own mastermind group, there are Internet sites that will help you for free, and most of them are associated through the work of Napoleon Hill. You need to ensure the group's commitment level is high because if some of the individuals don't participate on a continual basis the outcome is ineffective. When someone fails to participate it decreases the energy flow. If someone is unable to attend a meeting you should put a rule in place that they must notify the members prior to the meeting, and whoever is note taker can ensure they receive minutes of the meeting to keep them updated.

It takes a few meetings to form relationships and fully comprehend what each member is involved in. It is always helpful to send a picture and short bio of yourself to everyone in the group; this gives you a head start on forming relationships. You need to choose a time that will be effective for everyone, and sometimes that is a difficult choice due to the variances in time zones (especially if they are outside the United States).

Try to keep the size of the group between five and eight people. Choose people with the following qualities:

- Similar interests: likeminded; if you are a self-employed business owner you should seek others who have a similar background
- Similar success levels: this ensures continuity when seeking sound business advice
- Strong desire to succeed: they generally inspire you toward motivation and determination
- Supportive: usually passionate about life and career

Upon forming the team and coordinating a time and date (usually once/week—same day and time), someone needs to set up the phone conferencing (this can be done using freeconferencing.com). You will call in each week with the designated phone number and participant access code. You can also use Skype (which is no charge). Once you logon to the call, you designate the following:

- Leader: the leader oversees the meeting via assigning numbers relative to order of procession (as they call in, assign numbers accordingly), keeps things proceeding in an orderly fashion, reads the Master Mind principles at the beginning, and assigns duties for the next week.
- Note Taker: the note taker writes down minutes in a summarized manner and types and emails them to the group before the next meeting.
- Timekeeper: the timekeeper keeps the meeting moving so that each person has their specified timeframe for speaking. You allow one minute per person to announce their "wins" for the week, and the remainder

of the time is divided by how many people are on the call. Each call should last one hour.

Here are the Master Mind principles (to be read by the leader at the start of the group):

I RELEASE myself to the Master Mind because I am strong when I have others to help me.

I BELIEVE the combined intelligence of the Master Mind creates a wisdom far beyond my own.

I UNDERSTAND that I will more easily create positive results in my life when I am open to looking at myself and my problems and opportunities from another's point of view.

I DECIDE to release my desire totally in trust to the Master Mind and I am open to accepting new possibilities.

I FORGIVE myself for mistakes I have made. I also forgive others who have hurt me in the past so I can move into the future with a clean slate.

I ASK the Master Mind to hear what I really want, my goals, my dreams, my desires, and I hear my Master Mind partners supporting me in my fulfillment.

I ACCEPT: I know, relax, and accept, believing that the working power of the Master Mind will respond to my every need. I am grateful knowing this is so.

Dedication And Covenant

I now have a covenant in which it is agreed that the Master Mind shall supply me with an abundance of all things necessary to live a success-filled and happy life.

I dedicate myself to be of maximum service to God and my fellow human beings,

to live in a manner that will set the highest example for others to follow,

and to remain an open channel of God's will.

I go forth with a spirit of enthusiasm, excitement, and expectancy.

———————————

You are probably asking yourself how you could possibly benefit by forming a mastermind group. It is so empowering, and the things you receive can't be received with a college degree or measured by money. You gain a relationship that provides:

- Experience
- Skill
- Confidence
- Progression in your business and personal life
- Instant and valuable support network
- Opportunities for creating multiple sources of income
- Sense of shared endeavor
- Marketing
- Wealth of new ideas for solving existing problems and creating new growth and development

It is one of the best things you can do to propel you forward in your personal life and career.

Chapter 10
Fuel Your Growth With Zero-Gravity Relaxation

When we are no longer able to change a situation, we are challenged to change ourselves.
                    —Viktor E. Frankl

What we fear doing most is usually what we most need to do.
                    —Ralph Waldo Emerson

Revolutionizing your corporate life requires many steps. To become a successful leader you must eliminate certain aspects of your life, and in doing so you must first recognize where negative behavior comes from and then implement success principles to propel you to exponential growth. It is not an easy task, and hopefully I provided you with the tools and techniques to turn that negativity into positivity. Your personal life goes hand-in-hand with your professional career, and it is imperative that you find the balance.

In my teachings you come to recognize how everything works together and repetitiveness is key to acquiring success and happiness. When I discuss topics repetitively, they can have multiple meanings. Take, for instance, awareness. Awareness is about you as an individual; however, in the scope of things it is also relative to other people, your surroundings, your senses, and your circumstances.

I've also mentioned relaxation, which has many connotations. Throughout this book I have explained the positive impact relaxation has both personally and professionally. It affects your health and your growth. One of the relaxation methods I teach that is very effective is the zero gravity float experience.

Why do we float?

It assists you physically:

- Relieves stress
- Lowers high blood pressure
- Helps with rheumatism
- Relieves osteoarthritis
- Soothes muscular pain
- Reduces fatigue
- Improves fertility
- Helps eliminate migraine headaches

- Relieves symptoms of jet lag
- Lowers anxiety
- Decreases insomnia
- Soothes back pain
- Helps with depression
- Relieves premenstrual tension
- Relieves prenatal discomfort
- Helps with postnatal depression
- Reduces sleep disorders
- Improves recovery from injury
- Assists with fighting addiction
- Eliminates chronic pain
- Increases dopamine and endorphin levels
- Boosts mood and leaves you with a pleasant afterglow that lasts for days afterwards

It assists you spiritually:

- Everything you experience while floating comes from within yourself
- Creates time to reflect on your life, and reports of creative and personal insights abound
- Helps with meditation
- Places you in theta consciousness

It assists with learning and creativity:

- People have cut strokes off their golf game
- Developed complex scientific theories

- Composed music and drafted whole portions of books while floating
- With nothing to distract you, your level of creativity, concentration, and knowledge absorption is astonishing.

Kevin Johnson, Zero Gravity Institute, designed and built my float tank. He also educated me on all aspects of floating and has mastered the art of floating. Kevin is very well educated and invites me to share with you his findings: (http://zerogravityinstitute.com/introduction-to-floatation/): should you have any questions do not hesitate to reach out to him.

Floating and the Mind

When you change your body, you also change your mind. The reduced stimulation of the nervous system has a direct effect on the hypothalamus, the brain's chemical control center. Research has shown that internal events (thoughts and emotions) translate into measurable changes in body chemistry, and vice versa. The production of endorphins and the removal of undesirable chemicals during floating stimulate feelings of confidence, happiness and well-being, which helps you pursue your goals in life with maximum vitality and effectiveness. When floating, you achieve a level of physical relaxation, which is even deeper than sleep. In the flotation tank your mind remains awake and dreamily alert, just above the threshold of sleep. Large areas of the brain are suddenly liberated from their normal task of processing signals from the nervous system and organs. There is a sharp drop in the level of electrical activity of the brain (measured on an EEG) from the usual 20-25 Hz down to 4-8 Hz.; a slow, rhythmic wave pattern known as the theta state, or the "dream state."

For most people, the theta state is almost impossible to enter without falling asleep. In the tank you enter this elusive state effortlessly and enjoyably, and stay in it for most of the float session. This is a profound state of consciousness, a zone of inspirational thought processes and hyper creativity, where your learning abilities are at their highest and powers of visualization and auto-suggestion are greatly enhanced. Because your mind is freed from all external distractions during floating it can absorb new information quickly and on a very deep level. The learning process is accelerated by the theta state and by increased access to the efficient large-scale learning abilities of the right hemisphere.

EEG measurements on floaters show that the level of activity in the two hemispheres of the brain become more balanced and synchronized. This can produce a shift in awareness away from the normally dominant "left-brain" (logical, linear, analytical) towards the more intuitive, creative and large-scale specialties of the "right-brain." The tank does not inhibit the left hemisphere, but simply changes its role from one of dominance to one of cooperation with the other hemisphere, enabling floaters to use more of their cognitive potential. To fully exploit this mental potential, many modern flotation tanks are equipped with powerful underwater speakers and often with in-tank video. Any skill or information can be learned more effectively and efficiently while the floater is in a deep state of relaxation. Sophisticated audio or video based programs (such as SyberVision) can be used to guide the floater to peak performance in anything from language skills to golf swings. Learning has never been easier.

The mental and physical effects of floating profoundly improve your powers of emotional control and sense of well-being. Negative emotions and unwanted habits melt away in the tank along with the physical tensions and stresses that accompany them. Smoking, alcohol dependence and weight control problems can be easily and effectively overcome or lessened, sometimes totally spontaneously. Research suggests that compulsive behavior patterns such as these are linked to a low endorphin level in the body. In fact, according to experts at The National Institute of Mental Health, the float tank "is the only technique ever shown by controlled studies to be effective over extended periods of time." Studies show success rates of 81% in eliminating or sharply reducing smoking, 61% in reducing alcohol consumption, with similarly impressive results in combating weight control problems. In the deep theta state you have increased access to and control over subconscious mental processes. You become master of your own mind.

How it works:

It seems counterintuitive that something so simple could be so effective. But, scientists estimate that up to 90% of the brain's normal workload is caused by the effects of routine environmental stimulation, the combined effects of gravity, temperature, touch, light and sound on the muscles, nervous system and sense organs of the body. The floatation room screens out these external stimuli, creating a pure state of "sensory relaxation". Under these unique conditions your body has a chance to restore its natural powers of self-regulation, while you simply lie back and rediscover the latent abilities of a deeply relaxed mind.

The water/solution temperature is kept at a constant 93.5 degrees–relaxed skin temperature. As a result, the nerve endings, which cover the surface of the skin, no longer perceive a separation between the skin and the silky mineral solution, which surrounds it. In the dark, weightless tranquility of the Zero Gravity Float Room the boundaries of your body seem to dissolve and vanish. Because of the sharp reduction in signals being transmitted through the nervous system to the brain, you enter progressively deeper levels of relaxation. Your body seems to "disappear" from conscious awareness.

The sudden lack of stimulation to large areas of the nervous system triggers a spontaneous chain reaction throughout the body known as the parasympathetic response. Muscle tension, blood pressure, heart rate and oxygen consumption all drop dramatically. The entire chemistry of the body changes. The parasympathetic response is the body's natural mechanism for healing and regeneration. It can only occur during deep relaxation. Floating is the fastest, easiest, and most effective way of eliciting this response and enjoying its dramatic health benefits. Floating "resets" the body's chemical and metabolic balance, strengthening its resistance to the effects of stress, illness or injury.

Blood vessels including capillaries dilate, improving cardiovascular efficiency and increasing the supply of oxygen and nutrients to every cell in your body. This is called the vasodilatory effect. People who lead demanding lifestyles run the risk of developing high blood pressure, also known as hypertension. This disease has no symptoms, but eventually manifests itself in the form of strokes, heart attacks, and atherosclerosis (hardening of the arteries)—all potential killers. Floating can produce an immediate reduction in blood pressure and heart rate; regular floating may maintain this.

The endorphin is literally the essence of pleasure, sometimes called "the body's natural opiate". The endorphins released while floating create intense feelings of well-being, alleviating fatigue and chronic pain, as well as improving many of the higher brain functions such as memory and learning. The body's endorphin level is what makes some people naturally happy and others less so. Happiness is not an illusion– it is an endorphin.

Stress related chemicals such as adrenaline, cortisol, ACTH and lactate are removed from the bloodstream and replaced by beneficial endorphins. High levels of cortisol and ACTH are known to weaken the body's immune system and create feelings of depression, while lower baseline levels are associated with feelings of dominance and confidence. Apart from being the ultimate "stress buster", floating has been shown to alleviate asthma, arthritis, multiple sclerosis, gastrointestinal, and cardiovascular disorders. Tension related problems such as migraine, backache, and insomnia. These biochemical changes occur naturally and spontaneously as by-products of deep sensory relaxation. No special techniques or training are required. Just lie back and let it happen.

History of the Flotation Tank

In 1954, physician, neuroscientist and psychoanalyst Dr. John C. Lilly devised the flotation tank as part of his research at the National Institute of Mental Health. He was testing the premise that mental activity would cease in the absence of external stimuli. Instead, he found floating to be profoundly relaxing, and that it facilitated the discovery of richly elaborate states of inner experience. Since then, many people have discovered the multiple benefits of floating.

With more study and use by both researchers and the public, the initial terminology for flotation, "sensory deprivation", was changed to Restricted Environmental Stimulation Therapy. R.E.S.T. Therapy. With the research that followed came a greatly enhanced understanding of the many benefits for those who practice floatation. A great volume of published work continues to show improvements for users in managing stress, lowering blood pressure, reducing the presence of stress-related chemicals in the bloodstream, ceasing addictions, controlling chronic pain, enhancing creativity and mental acuity, among other known benefits.

Such studies and their results merely confirm what veteran floaters have known for years—floating is a natural, healthy way to relax and rejuvenate. Meanwhile, floating has caught on in America, Australia and, more recently, Asia and Europe as a powerfully productive and creative form of recreation in its own right.

We've covered a lot of ground in these pages, and I encourage you to embrace relaxation and meditation to help declutter your mind as you seek balance in your personal and professional lives. Go ahead, place yourself in that surreal surrounding. Coaching and relaxation are a winning combination to reach success and happiness and to help you—

REVOLUTIONIZE YOUR CORPORATE LIFE!

About The Author

Peggy Caruso is a certified executive and personal development coach, author and 8-time entrepreneur.

Her 'Revolutionize' series has been approved as a trademark and inclusive of that are her previous books, *"Revolutionize Your Life"* and *"Revolutionize Your Child's Life."* Her current book, *"Revolutionize Your Corporate Life"* is a resource guide for anyone in the business arena.

Peggy has been interviewed by 50+ radio stations across the U.S. and Canada and has been interviewed by many TV stations.

She is committed to assisting individuals both personally and professionally.

References

Dr. Robert Anthony, www.thesecretodeliberatecreation.com

Genevieve Behrend, author of *Your Invisible Power*, www.yourinvisiblepowerfree.com

Jack Canfield, author, motivational speaker, www.jackcanfield.com

Napoleon Hill, Napoleon Hill Foundation, author of *Think and Grow Rich*, 1937. www.naphill.org

Kevin Johnson, Zero Gravity Institute, www.zerogravityinstitute.com

Dr. Steve G. Jones, hypnotherapist, NLP trainer, author, www.stevegjones.com

Dr. Joseph Murphy, www.drjosephmurphy.com

Earl Nightingale, author of *The Strangest Secret*

Kevin Johnson, www.zerogravityinstitute.com

Price Pritchett, author of *You2*, www.pricepritchett.com

Bob Proctor, business consultant, motivational speaker, personal development coach, author, star of the movie *The Secret*. www.bobproctorcoaching.com

Wallace Wattles, author of *The Science of Getting Rich*

A free eBook edition is available with the purchase of this book.

To claim your free eBook edition:

1. Download the Shelfie app.
2. Write your name in upper case in the box.
3. Use the Shelfie app to submit a photo.
4. Download your eBook to any device.

Shelfie

A free eBook edition is available
with the purchase of this print book.

CLEARLY PRINT YOUR NAME ABOVE IN UPPER CASE

Instructions to claim your free eBook edition:
1. Download the Shelfie app for Android or iOS
2. Write your name in **UPPER CASE** above
3. Use the Shelfie app to submit a photo
4. Download your eBook to any device

Print & Digital Together Forever.

Snap a photo

Free eBook

Read anywhere

Morgan James makes all of our titles available
through the Library for All Charity Organizations.

www.LibraryForAll.org

Printed in the USA
CPSIA information can be obtained
at www.ICGtesting.com
JSHW082343140824
68134JS00020B/1841